Pinnies and Pegs:
A Gypsy Childhood

by Ryalla Duffy

Publisher Robert Dawson

Pinnies and Pegs:
A Gypsy Childhood

Published by Robert Dawson, 2009
188 Alfreton Road, Blackwell
Alfreton, Derbys DE55 5JH

ISBN **978-1-903418-64-2**

Unusual words or concepts in the text have been starred and are explained in the Romani and notes at the end.

The decorative motifs on either side of the chapter headings are designs used for traditional harness furniture.

Printed by 4 Sheets Design and Print Ltd
Prospect Farm, Manor Road, South Wingfield, Alfreton, DE55 7NH

Introduction

Pinnies and Pegs, which is loosely autobiographical, could as easily have been entitled ramblings from a perambulator or ponderings from a push chair. It is a modest collection of early memories, impressions, and accounts of events which have been passed on and retold over the years. Little cameos of happenings, threaded together like beads on a string. For this reason, the reader may from time to time protest that this didn't happen just this way, or such and a body wasn't exactly like that. Some names have been changed to afford privacy, others have not.

Pinnies and Pegs invites you on a Gypsy journey from birth to babyhood and beyond. Many of our family photographs fell victim to fire and flood over the years, but I have shared with you some of those which remain.

Looking back over half a century of Travelling life, those early years were simple and austere. Therein, on reflection, lies their richness. I have been blessed with many children and grandchildren and one of my reasons for writing this book was so that they may have some record of their past and their history. Later generations will only marvel at the freedom we enjoyed then. We still have horses and waggons today, and continue to enjoy a meal cooked outside on a stick fire. Legislation has curtailed many aspects of Travelling life but the spirit remains strong. Long may it be so.

My thanks are also extended to the following people who have helped and supported both this book and my written work over the years: Bob Dawson (Publisher), Janet Dawson (Childcare), Siobhan Spencer (DGLG), Jenny Boyd-Cropley (Cottage Books), Pat Ingal (Traveller Education Service), Olga Sinclaire, Juliette de Bairacli-Levy, Alan E Jones, Mike Barrett.

I would like to dedicate this book to my family. They have shaped my past, present and future, a small link in a long chain.

1
Pinnies and Pegs

The first my Mam knew about my impending birth was when she had a grave encounter with a runaway horse and cart.

Whether she was attempting to stop the animal or whether she never noticed its thundering approach, she was unable to recall, having been rendered unconscious on impact and then hastily transferred to the local cottage hospital.

When she finally came to, battered bruised, bandaged and bemused, the white coated pipe-smoking doctor pronounced her condition as being satisfactory. He stressed "condition" so pointedly and punctuated it with smoke, that my Mam made further enquiries, nearly verging on a relapse when informed that she was "with child" and a baby would soon be making an appearance.

My dad absorbed the announcement with a wry smile and a few extra inhalations of pigtail twist — in common with the Doctor, he was also an enjoyer of nicotine! Taking refuge in a pungent cloud of smoke, he pondered on the improbability of this new turn of events.

When the haze subsided, so had the shock of imminent fatherhood and he walked off into the distance with his long dogs, whistling thoughtfully and pondering on the changes that lay ahead.

I was born in the gentle spring of 1959, apple blossom time, in the Vale of Evesham.

Because of Mam's "funny age" (forty plus) and the recent horse and cart episode, the midwife insisted on a hospital delivery in case of complications.

Mercifully there weren't any and my Mam even managed to have her baby "born on the straw" in line with ancient Romany custom, a practise which sadly is dying out in recent times, probably due to the diluting of the race with over much "gorgia"* blood.

An early hospital discharge was agreed, providing that the midwife could make home visits on a regular basis.

Mam agreed, anything to escape the confines of the hospital.

With hindsight, she may not have acquiesced so readily, had she fully realised, how 'regularly', would be!

In those days, Social Services hadn't been invented and the address of "no fixed abode" always flagged up attention.

The midwife's concerns lessened little on learning that "home" was a horse drawn caravan with water sourced from the church yard tap and cooking being done outside over a stick fire.

Country midwives were used to Gypsy ways, their services often not called for at all or only after the event.

Mam's midwife was city born and unused to Romany custom. She took a dim view of these heathen domestic arrangements. It became a personal crusade on her part to ensure my survival and to this end she would make local enquiries as to our family's whereabouts.

The ringing of the bell would herald her arrival, which in turn set all the dogs off barking.

Puffing, perspiring and pedalling hard, her uniformed bosom heaving with exertion, she'd skid to an unexpected halt trilling. "Ai've found you," triumphantly.

Dad would disappear in yet another haze of pipe smoke until her departure — avoiding "a women's things" like the plague and only warily reappearing when assured of her departure. He distrusted all bodies in uniforms, whatever their gender.

Mam tolerated Nurse Woodberry's visits solely on account of the contents of her bicycle basket. Home-made cake and jam always made an appearance and later matinee jackets and other knitted apparel. Despite a similar inbred distrust of authority to that of my Dad, Mam developed a grudging admiration for Woodberry's tenacity and fortitude and Dad developed a liking for her cake.

On occasions, a local constable would make an appearance, intent on moving us on. In situations like this, Woodberry came into her own, making a formidable ally. Legs apart and arms akimbo, she would block the officer's path, uniform to uniform and toe to toe, repelling the unwarranted intruder.

No-one ever got past the bosom on the bike, regardless of reason or rank!

Afterwards, there would be a conspiratorial cup of tea to celebrate her success.

At the time, Mam never questioned the "Woodberry's" dedication to duty, but in later years we came to realise her calling was a true vocation.

With no husband or children of her own and a generous heart, we somehow filled a gap in her life. The lot of a childless spinster in the 1960s — of which there seemed to be a profusion — could be a cheerless one. Looking back, for a childless one, I always thought midwifery to be a strange choice of occupation, similar to always being the bridesmaid but never being the bride.

The spring of 1959 turned briskly to summer and I spent my days in my Mam's arms or in a large but battered "Silver Cross" pram of which I was one in a long line of less than careful previous owners. The one time Rolls Royce of the perambulator world, it played a vital role in Mam's attempts at domestic arrangements, assuming the role of second car — not that we had a first car. My dad had a horse and spinner — a two wheeled horse drawn cart — but the Silver Cross was exclusively Mam's conveyance, serving to transport churns of water, shopping, firewood, drunken husbands and even, occasionally, babies.

Gypsy women did quite a trade in those days in *pram chopping**, dealing up and down for a newer model depending on their finances at the time.

It gave a whole new meaning to "wheels to work". Most families owned a pram regardless of whether of not they owned a child.

Mornings I awoke to bird song, skylarks and goldfinches chorusing in harmony. Wood smoke drifting from a stick fire and the chink chink of the horses' tether chain as they moved to graze. In the distance, there always seemed to be a dog barking or the chiming of a church bell to intimate the time of day.

The Vale of Evesham was home to much of the Midlands food production, serving large populations in cities like "Brum".

Dairy farms were common, providing milk and meat and a wealth of vegetables and fruit was grown in the rich and fertile soil of the Vale.

This needed harvesting and preparing for market, all labour intensive occupations for the mobile workforce of Gypsy families.

Hearing on the grapevine — mobile phones were unthought of then — of a farm offering land work, Dad would bicycle over to the landowner in question to ascertain the likelihood of being able to

pull-in for a while and the rates of pay being offered. If the conditions were favourable — Dad was known to 'cut his nose off to spite his face' — if they weren't he'd be home in half the time it had taken him to get there, urging Mam to get a shift on and pack-down while he "got a move on" and "yoked up".

Dogs would be tied to the back of the waggon and the remains of the outside fire stamped out. Bantams were reluctantly captured from their scratching and in little or no time, we'd be "jallin' the drom" again and on the road to pastures new, leaving behind nothing but wood ash from the fire and droppings from the horses or a few wood shavings if Dad had been in the mood to make a few pegs.

From my wobbly vantage point on the bunk bed at the back of the waggon I had a wide view, through the open door, over the horse's back, to the road stretching temptingly ahead. Conversely, it was possible to look through the little window at the back of the waggon and contemplate the passing countryside which we were leaving behind, two tell-tale white bands on the road laying testimony to the route we had taken as the iron shod wheels made contact with the metalled surface of the road. No need for *patrins** if the trail was fresh and the horses had had a good feed. Many was the house-holder who followed hopefully in our wake with a bucket and shovel intent on blessing his roses!

May blossom and cow-parsley, more delicately described as "old ladies lace", vied with cascades of pale dog roses blushing pink and fragile on their stem. Verges vibrant with purple vetch and fragrant meadow sweet were home to butterflies and bees.

An occasional Morris Minor or Austin Cambridge would honk its horn, irritated by the delay on the narrow road that Dad's slow three-mile-an-hour progress had caused.

Eventually, a field gateway would hove into view and the horse and waggon swing wide to take a bumpy turn through the rutted gateway, to pull up along the sheltering hedge-side.

Even at such an early stage of life, there is an inexplicable excitement on arriving at a new *atchin-tan**, especially if it has been left pristine and unsullied by previous occupants, as was frequently the case with land-work stopping places.

One of my earliest and most abiding memories is the smell of crushed camomile that always seemed to favour growing round the sandy much disturbed soil of such gateways.

While Mam held the shafts and the cob was unyoked, I'd be lifted down to pull dry sticks from the hedge ready for the lighting of the first fire.

When the horse was tethered and the collar and harness laid to let the sweat dry, Dad would blow flames to the sticks and hang a sooty kettle from the *kekauvi-saster**

Dogs would be free to scour the fresh enticing vicinity for rabbits and our splattering of bantams, released from enforced captivity to dust bathe and scratch, shaking the remains of indignity from their journey! Their industrious and unwavering search for food assured a supply of fresh eggs for the following morning.

It has always been a source of magic to me, the speed at which Travellers can set up or pack down a camp. It takes very little time or effort for the rudimentary elements of a home to be in place. How their close affinity with their animals provided nearly all their dietary requirements. Dogs hunting for hares and rabbits, bantams providing meat and eggs, cobs supplying pulling power and even a nanny goat, for the supply of fresh milk.

Probably the only downside of this healthful fare was the vast supplies of white bread, white sugar and huge quantities of fat bacon that were consumed.

With harness stowed on the cratch, protected from varmints and weather, and china and candlesticks unpacked in the wagon, another shiftin' had successfully been accomplished.

There's a special intuition that Travellers seem to have about the coming and going of other families. A deep unfathomable racial "knowing" of knowledge. I believe the lack of literacy has kept this ability especially keen and for that reason education of children has always been viewed as the harbinger of mixed blessings.

Even before the kettle had boiled and while the waggon was still being unpacked from its travels, a neighbouring family would happen by and a sprinkling of bodies arrive magnetically.

A Nice little old spot you's got here though ain't it... have yous pulled in for the pickin' then?

"Hope 'e pays better than the place we'm too... 'e's as tight as a gnat's arse, the old *beng** we'm a *bootying** for..."

"Ain't it a life eh,... still there's not much about for the like's o' we so what can you do?"

As dusk fell "dimsie dark" and the sun threatened to set, its scarlet departure impending, conversation rose and fell and I'd drift into sleep, secure, safe and trusting in my babyhood world.

Sun rose early in those halcyon summer days, the dawn chorus nature's alarm clock. Mist cleared slowly to reveal Bredon Hill or the Malvern Hills in the blue and hazy distance. Unhurried and unchanging, solid, ancient and blessedly dependable landmarks, from which those familiar with them could get their bearings and navigate a route to their desired destination.

Somewhere nearby, out of sight but not of smell, a herd of morning milkers, maidens of the meadow would wend a leisurely and udder heavy procession to the cow-man to relieve themselves of their dairy delights. Maternal mooing accompanied their swaying motion, the odour of fresh dung pervasive in the damp air.

Water being a scarce commodity, ablutions were mercifully restricted to a lick and a promise in only a suggestion of soapy water. A wet comb pulled through the hair implied styling. I usually received the lick and the last one to be washed the promise!

Other families would arrive spasmodically, along with the farmer who would know most of the workers by name — not usually their real ones.

Instructions would be given for the task ahead and older children threatened or coaxed into giving a hand. The threatening and coaxing technique on the little ones gave a poor return for the energy expended... "God blind 'is eyes 'h'em the laziest little cusser wot you's ever had misfortune to set eyes on, God strike me dead iffen 'e aint", a mother would exclaim, squinting proudly at her wayward offspring.

While babies were strapped in prams with dummies and biscuits for company, those able to walk, set about playing in the loamy soil near their parents, sampling or trampling the crop as inclination took them. "'E'm a right little bastard ain't he though", would be inquired of those spectators in ear-shot.

Peas and strawberries were a favourite item to be harvested and small moist mouths could consume vast amounts in-between gurgles and smiles, with no apparent disruption to the digestive system. ÆE'll go an gid 'is-self the shits afore the day is out, take a dying oath iffen 'e dont."

With these dire foretellings ringing in small ears, the recent "licks and promises" became distant memories as shoes were discarded and cotton frocks assumed a familiar matt grubbiness.

Ribbons and bows were wrenched from tousled curls by chubby fingers and those too young to have embraced the concept of being dry, allowed a warm stream of piddle to traverse down dimpled legs, leaving a tell-tale trickle down sun browned dusty skin.

For the fortunate few, or not, (the days of the disposable diaper not yet thought of) the terry towelling and plastic elasticated pants were in vogue. A dubious blessing at the best of times, they boasted low levels of absorbency and high levels of discomfort for the unfortunate wearer. The risk of chaffing and the preservation of high levels of ammonia caused many a toddler to sport... "an arse like a baboon... God love 'im".

"Is it time for a fag yet my Genti" was the mid morning cry.

"I'm as dry as me granny's", came the delightful reply.

"Who's mashin' the *meskie**?"

"On me blessed baby's life me back is broke in two"

"This field's wusser than the last one we was to."

General admissions of discomfort would herald a retreat from the field to the welcome shade of a nearby hawthorn hedge. Loose tea leaves added directly to a boiling blackened kettle followed by the hasty addition of "coronation" milk. Carnation milk, to give it it's real name, was the mainstay of many Travellers diets, sporting a red and white label with the appropriate flower motif embossed on the can, closely followed in popularity by its competitor in trade Ideal Milk, in an eye-catching blue and white stripped tin.

Without the fridges and chillers of today, fresh bottled milk rapidly turned sour. Condensed or evaporated milk, with two holes pierced in the can top to ease the flow of contents, was the forerunner in convenience food. There was also a pre-sweetened variety with sugar already added which proved even more convenient!

Despite the dire warning on the label advising against its use for feeding infants, the information being lost on customers not schooled in literacy, large quantities were liberally used to fill "titty" bottles and the contents drunk without any apparent harm to the infants concerned. In later years, many dentists would probably make a handsome living from those raised and weaned on the sugared variety!

With tea made, white bakers' loaves made an appearance from wicker baskets, buttered at one end then clamped dexterously under the arm and sliced in one deft movement to waiting out stretched hands. Bread was taken swiftly with the portion touched by hand left uneaten and discarded as *mokadi** and thrown to the dogs.

Groups disappeared to the privacy of long grass to relieve themselves of excesses of tea in readiness for the next stint on the field. Crumbs were dusted off, and babies attended to and resettled. Titty bottles replenished with the last of the cooled tea, and calls made to the reluctant to return to the task in hand.

Cigarettes and expletives punctuated the air, the reduction in enthusiasm palpable, conveyed in weary grimaces and knowing grins. Salty suggestiveness across the rows degenerated into rich and descriptive crudity, uniting the Travellers with a shared appreciation of the earthy humour and diverting minds from tired muscles.

Dry wit has long been at the fore in the Travellers' armoury of survival techniques. Laughter is, after all, free and weights no pockets, benefiting the more from being shared.

Some of the women feigned shock and disapproval unconvincingly, to anyone who took notice.

Harvesting determination and dexterity the toiling continued through the noon day heat. Piece work is a natural motivator, however and many families relied on money earned in the summer months to see them through the "starve-belly" winter months.

Be it turnip hoeing or pea-picking, strawberries or spuds, a tally was kept of earnings and a watchful eye kept by the farmer or tallyman returning in the afternoon to pay out what was owed. Workers were skilled in the art of adjusting matters in their favour by a cunning variety of means.

Water and stones added to weight and carelessly picked harvests could be cosmeticed into looking marketable by placing carefully picked items artistically on top. "Cor, you's aint half agonna cop it iffen the old *mush* diks** ya"; "Gotta dik me though first ain 'e...." was a much heard exchange.

As the day drew to a close, weary wilting workers would thankfully head for home, still making light of the day.

"Make sure an' leave some for the likes 'o we in the morning."

"Iffen I wins the pools or me bonds come up, yous can 'av my share tomorrow."

"Ain it a life though, on me dear ol mother's life, me back is broke".

Clambering into a motley variety of rarely roadworthy pick-ups and vans, cabs filled to overflowing with dusky passengers, the vehicles bumped and lurched through the rutted gateway and out onto the road. A fanfare of spasmodic honking and hooting marked their departure.

2
Paisley and Plaid

Although my Mam and Dad enjoyed the company and undeniable exchange of wit, there was a perceptible sigh of relief when once again they had the delightful dusk of the field to themselves.

The dogs once again relaxed lethargically into the hedge bottom and the bantam trio emerged from a nearby tree where they had temporarily been forced to take refuge from the unwanted attentions of Elias John and Moses Eli, two handsome small boys who were uncannily good shots with homemade catapults.

Back at the waggon, more dry wood was pulled from the hedgerow, and a greaseproof bread bag added to the embers soon had the kettle preparing to boil.

Dad would strip to the waist and wash down in cold water, then reknot his *diklo** and re-comb his hair, finishing off with a smear of brylcream and a final twist of his fingers to produce a jaunty quiff.

Mam had the "top of the kettle" by now half warmed — and washed me and then herself. Lifebuoy or Wrights Coal Tar always seemed to feature in the process. I was glad we had to fetch all our water from some distance, as it meant washing was kept to the bare minimum.

Dad usually located a cattle trough or a fast running stream for all but drinking water.

Each morning he'd set off with his long dogs at heel, to fetch fresh supplies, so Mam could "dab a bit o washing out" before the day got going. In summer months, it was dry by teatime and smelt of the hedgerow and sunshine, although it never attained pristine whiteness, content to settle for humbler shades of grey.

While Mam set about preparing food for her family, a bucket would be set aside by the embers and a generous shake of Omo or Daz flakes mixed in. Sometimes, in a rare fit of efficiency "dolly blue" would be added to the cocktail to bring the whiteness out — it must have been a long search however, without guarantee of success. Eventually most of Mam's "whites" gave up the ghost and turned grey, albeit a whiter shade of grey.

Up to her elbows in suds, Mam would wring and rub till she had worked up as greater lather as her laundry and the water had turned a satisfying black. Her efforts were then cast on the nearest bramble bush, she'd done her bit! We tried to dissuade her from attempting woollens — once they had encountered her ministrations they were never the same again. Her intentions were honourable and jumble sales frequent.

Nearly every Saturday, women who had not managed to clothe their families by means of *monging** at the door, would board a Midland Red bus and congregate outside some village hall. Payment of 6d would gain admission including tea and biscuits. Once the doors opened a beeline would be made for "Travellerified" apparel. Particular favourites included paisleys and plaids, polka dots and stripes — the more garish and mismatched the better.

Someone always unearthed a corset of gargantuan proportions and would wave it shamelessly aloft to a chorus of sniggers and wolf whistles. The young women voiced scorn and derision — searching for "baby-dolls", a rather racy and in vogue, though highly impractical, hip-high negligee and knicker type outfit, guaranteed to get even the slowest male pulse racing — or so the wearers hoped!!

Bags and baskets full, customers resorted to refreshment at rickety green baize card tables and partook of rich tea biscuits dunked in tepid Typhoo.

"Iffen this *meskie** as *dikked** tealeaves, it musta bin a long time ago, 'tis like witches' piss, take a dying oath iffen it ain't."

"That pale it's fit to faint I shouldn't wonder."

"Poverty ol place this, an a church hall at that, theys wouldn't give yous the steam off their...." added Pemberline hopefully, though completely out of context.

Once home, having shared a packet of Woodbines and a Fisherman's Friend on the back seat, an impromptu fashion parade would ensue at the roadside camp, giving budding devas the chance to admire their tastes in fashion. No-body owned a mirror so the effect was judged according to the comments of observers.

"Mutton dressed as lamb and no mistake."

"Red hat and no drawers... it matches your *yoks**... bloodshot."

"Fits where it touches an' it don't touch much..."

"My blessed dear lord, yous ain't never going to be seen a-wearing that get-up."

"Now I sees this an it takes me fancy... I'm going to give my Jimmy a good time tonight, yous see iffen I don't."

"Take your fancy... it'll tickle your fancy brazen face."

Travellers' clothing styles are easily recognisable yet intangible and for the older generations the addition of the "horseshoe pinny" completed the ensemble. These large half-circle shaped wraparound garments sported two large pockets for storage and a hefty frill round the hem with apron strings that tied at the back.

I never saw my Mam wear trousers, neither did she wear stockings, which was probably a disappointment for my dad.

Once, in a rare moment of vanity, she tried out a new invention called a "roll-on," which didn't do what it said on the tin. The Trades Descriptions Act hadn't been invented then or it would have been re-christened The Struggle On. After much cussing and sweating whilst she stepped into it and tried to summon the strength to tug it up to waist height, the obnoxious garment was finally in place, much to the delight of female onlookers who cheered at the achievement.

"My dear Blessed Lord, you's am trussed like a *kanni**, Blessed Lord strike me dead if you ain't."

"It'll tek some *mush** to work his way through that bugger."

Needless to say, the desired effect was not achievable and bulges were merely displaced, only to reappear at either end of the elastic tube, creating a lop-sided three tier torso effect.

Despite public derision and no small degree of discomfort, mam persevered for almost a week, by which time the "roll-on" was wrinkled and grey. Determined to rectify this grubby condition she decided to give it the boil wash treatment. Her horror can only be imagined as, plunging it into the steaming suds, it was seen to be writhing and contorting beyond recognition as the elastic encountered the heat, bearing a marked resemblance to a cow's stomach.

"I'd *del** that to the *juks** if I was you," was the closest my dad got to sympathy. Needless to say it was the first and last foundation garment our family clapped eyes on.

Women were barelegged most of the time but the wearing of boots was common. Buckskin side buttoned boots held a particular charm, as did those of Spanish leather.

Hair was kept long, but not loose. Loose hair signified loose morals. Plaiting and braiding was popular, as were ringlets and kiss-curls. Often hair was oiled or sugared into place. Sugar water combed through the locks set them into place all day long, though

there was a risk of attracting the wrong kind of attention from bees and wasps.

Adornments were rudimentary, tortoise shell side combs and kirkby-grips being common. Rubber-bands held braids in place, bound round with ribbons and bows or a scrap of lace.

Women in their seventies and eighties sported fine sets of plaits and indeed, even today, I know octogenarians who are proud of their ringlets. For the young and trendy girls beehives and back-combing were in vogue but Mam resisted these innovations and contented herself with the odd splash of peroxide to "emphasise her highlights', some phrase out of Woman's Own of which she did not know the meaning.

Mostly we did hair washing only when it rained, collecting rain water in vessels for the soaping and rinsing, its natural softness leaving hair smooth and shining. Vinegar would be added to the final rinse. The effect was good but the smell held less appeal. Lemon juice was sometimes used in its stead.

All but the poorest Gypsy women sported some good quality heavy items of gold, rings or bangles, earrings or chains. Sovereigns, crowns and dollars were much sought after. Pawn and second hand shops regularly merited a visit to inspect their stock. By word of mouth and reputation, most Travellers knew which establishments would trade in the types of merchandise they favoured and who would and would not be prepared to "have a deal". Some of the less well-off families would be forced to request that an item be put by and paid off at so much a week until the required sum was reached.

Travellers of a higher class paid cash there and then and had the well deserved pleasure of taking their purchases away with them, often with added discount for an immediate cash sale. In point of fact, a good bout of haggling between vendor and pur-chaser is a joy to behold. Much showmanship and persistence is required.

"What I is a-going to tell 'e is the Gods honest truth, may the dear Lord strike me dead iffen it ain't."

"On my baby Lena's life, baby die iffen I dain't tell the truth."

Contorting of facial expression and pleas of appeal to onlookers, along with wild gesticulation and forecasts of doom and bravado are delivered at length and with startling intensity, interchanged with feigned shock, horror and disinterest.

"I've already turned down, 's.... once today, but I've a kind heart and I like to do a body a good turn when I can."

"Believe yous me yous'll regret it sumink terrible iffen yous don't take this hopportunity wot the dear Lord has brought your way. Yous couldn't buy it nowhere for what I'm a hofferin it yous for an I tek a oath on me mothers grave."

"Well please yourself, I can sell these times over, take an oath if I can't."

Some items of gold were bespoke pieces executed by highly skilled goldsmiths. This, added to the extreme weight of the gold itself, made them highly valuable. Even babies and small children prided themselves on miniature replicas of the styles popular with their parents. Little double-buckle and keeper rings, bent sovereigns, and horses heads could all be seen adorning chubby dimpled fingers. Babes in arms would then and still now, sport solid gold "dummies" on chunky belcher chains. Proud symbols of wealth, worn by children so precious that no expense was spared.

This in stark contrast to the fact that often children's clothes were begged, borrowed, cut-down or handed-down. The fate of footwear fared little better, the most affluent of Travellers making visits to the cities to purchase patent "startrights" with a cutaway heel.

The rest of us had sandals in the summer and wellingtons in the winter — as evidenced by the tell-tale red rings a few inches below the knee where the rubber had chaffed without mercy. As if this wasn't indignity enough, pride delved to new depths when Dad employed his "cobbling" skills.

In his thrifty opinion, money spent on shop bought shoes was an expenditure outside of our income bracket. It was left to Mam's cadging skills to provide a solution. When asked what size I took Mam would helpfully impart "Anything between a 1 and a 4"

I would cringe with dread as outdated and impractical footwear was offered for inspection. On the way home, I'd shuffle along in models too big, or blister my way home in models too small. Dad's cobbling led to my hobbling.

With the aid of a razor, he'd cut the leather toes clean out of tight shoes giving the open-toe effect — often with a generous overhang.

With leather, tacks and "clickety segs", worn down heels would be raised and I'd be left making more noise walking along a pavement than a tap-dancer on speed, drawing unwelcome attention from passers-by in my outlandish footwear. In a vain attempt to soothe my annoyance, Mam would helpfully chip in with "the leather's good quality, you'll soon grow into them — bet they cost a pretty penny when they were new... all they need is a lick o' polish." However, there are some wrongs even Cherry Blossom can't right.

3
Grinding
for the Queen

My first summer, like most in those days, was a leisurely one, spent almost entirely out of doors.

Rural England in the 1960s had a grace and favour of its own, made precious by its relative simplicity and predictability. Many of the farms we stopped on still worked the land with horse power and those that had moved onto tractor power still had old faithfuls pensioned in paddocks, Shires and Clydesdales with dinner plate hooves, heavily feathered and broad chests below power shoulders. These gentle giants that had ploughed furrows with rhythmic pace and patient skill, fertilising as they worked.

Often when toiling in pocket handkerchief pastures, we would come across rusted iron horseshoes long lost but bearing testament to their owners' contribution to husbandry.

For us, there was the frequent "shifting", as either we moved, or other families pulled on or pulled off. Field work offered frequent pull-ins, a steady income and a hectic social life. At odd times there'd be a trip into town or a ride on a Midland Red into Worcester, Evesham or Kidderminster known affectionately as "Kiddy". Returning home with delicacies such as black pudding (Dad's treat) fresh faggots, double diamond cheese or tubs of dripping, packed in Mam's basket or overflowing into brown paper carrier bags with white string handles which cut the fingers with the ease of a cheese wire.

Nobody had fridges in those days so purchases were eaten almost immediately, before they went off. If there was a stream nearby they'd be wrapped in a "muslim" (muslin), then set in a lidded bucket in the shallows — this extended the life of some products, but not for long. Apart from *Gypsy Cakes** — scone-like creations rolled flat and cooked on a griddle or hoop-handled frying pan, then eaten hot with butter, Mam never baked. For a start, she didn't have an oven. Cakes and such were a great weak-

ness of my old Dad's, maybe as a result of all the rationing and shortages he'd experienced during the war. Returning from a shopping session, he'd greet us with a mashing of tea, in eager anticipation of one of his favourites having been purchased. Cream horns infused with cream and sprinkled with sugar, vanilla slices crested with icing and thick with custard or lardy cakes, sticky treats with dried fruit encased in fatty dough curls always caused him to break into a toothy grin. Mam would keep him on tenterhooks. declaring herself "fair parched" and packing away her purchases in the pan-box, all the while knowing he'd be keeping a beady eye on her fast emptying basket.

As he made the tea, she'd attempt to fob him off with pigs' trotters or tripe which in turn he'd dismiss impatiently with an "ar very nice". Finally the desired confection would materialise and he'd be happy to admit, "I sees you's ain't forgot me after all". A man of few words, and those he did have "saved for best'! This little game between them re-enacted ritually on each occasion.

We always had bought bread, white crusty loaves, springy to the touch — at least for a while. On subsequent days it'd be sliced and browned on the embers then spread with dripping or Echo margarine. My Dad would also, in hard times, of which there seemed to be many, eat it spread with lard and a sprinkling of salt and pepper.

Apart from store-bought ice-cream, frozen food wasn't on the market for most. Vegetables and fruit were eaten in season and habitually sourced from the nearest field or market garden. Meat was caught with the aid of a lurcher or bought from the local butcher who still hung produce up outside the shop to attract local flies and be prodded squeezed and coughed on by passers by.

Home cured bacon withstood the test of time and could be sliced at will and rewrapped in "muslims" for weeks at a time. It made a frequent appearance for breakfast with eggs, and later at teatime with boiled spuds and cabbage. Tinned food made occasional appearances, with salmon for Sundays and sardines for Mondays. Tinned peaches partnered tinned cream, which bore no resemblance to the fresh variety. Luncheon meat was the manufacturers' answer to post war austerity. Nauseously pink in colour and boasting little flavour, its texture had a quality which defied classification or replication, and few wished to try. Last but not least, corned beef, in strange shaped tins with a key glued on top, specifically designed to slice through the users finger when attempting to free the containers contents. A not so tempting serving suggestion added a dash of piccalilli, though not a repast for the faint of heart as it was rumoured to repeat on the consumer!

Many families passed through the Vale of Evesham. Stanleys, Lees, Smiths, Taylors, and Prices. Another local family were the Scarrats and they were regular visitors, many of them red-headed like myself, suffering taunts of "Scarrats, Scarrats, hair like carrots". Their children and I would go into battle against the tormenting tactics of village children, invariably emerging as victors — until the next encounter.

Many's the time the coloured ribbons Mam lovingly attached to my curls were wrenched without reason from my head — taking generous clumps of hair with them on account of how tightly the knots had been tied to avoid them falling out and being lost.

It was years before I forgave my hair for all the trouble it got me into!

Now, so many years later, seeing one of my grand-daughters,

Tiger-Lily, with the same devilishly delightful red curls that once crowned my head, I wonder whether she will suffer the same fate. If that proves to be the case, I am hopeful that she will deal with those that tease in the way they so justly deserve. Knowing her spirit I think my wishes may yet prove to be fulfilled! She wasn't called Tiger for nothing.

There's not a Gypsy child walking who's not endured taunts of "Gyppo" at one time or another. These remarks, now acknowledged as racist, clearly emphasise how early the demarcation between Gypsy and *gorgia* are made. Once the line has been drawn it is usually irreversible and the attitudes of distrust are life-long thus perpetuating the limbo land on the fringes of society where the Travelling community find itself existing.

We also had family stopping round the Forest of Dean but in those days the distance between the Forest and the Vale was too great to be reasonably traversed regularly. Though we had news of them via the "Travellers' Telegraph", they may as well have been "stopping" on the moon. With no postal address, meagre literacy skills, no telephone and little motor transport, it is easy to understand how families fell out of touch, only getting belated news of births and deaths via word of mouth or many mouths. By the time it reached its destination, such information as was received was either hopelessly out of date or riddled with inaccuracies due to the series of Chinese whispers that the facts had been subjected to.

My Mam's family were originally Prices. Somewhere in the distant past, her Mam (my maternal Granny) had married a wheelwright and coach builder from Yorkshire whose income was supplemented with waggon building and repair. On one occasion, when the Prices had come to collect and pay for work which they had commissioned, my Granny Ethel, who was little more than a "strip of a lass", had caught the wheelwright's eye.

After much deliberation, my Great Granny Price, having estimated the wheelwright's income and social standing, and considering him to be what we would these days term "a bit of a wideo", encouraged the liaison.

Doubtless she was also gauging the financial benefit of having a son-in law who was handy with a spoke shave! While the Prices debated the matter and little Ethel's future hung in the balance, it came to their notice that Ethel's beau was somewhat skilled in the art of bare fist fighting. Having kinship to Black Billy Price, another fair booth fighter, they decided this contributory factor would clinch their decision and so the marriage went ahead. Whether Ethel was entirely enamoured of this turn of events is somewhat unclear, but possibly she was not as thrilled at the prospect as her mother. What is known is that relations with her and Great Granny were forever after strained and I do not think she ever fully forgave her mother, thinking up ways to get her own back, the primary one being the fact that she was now "a cut above the rest".

Now that I have some grasp of history and not wishing to judge Great Granny's motives, having never had the chance to meet her, I do ponder on whether or not the great war of 1914/1918 had some part to play in the decision she made. Was there a shortage of eligible young Gypsies? Certainly many gave their lives for king and country in both the first and second world wars. My own Mam always said she was born in the same year that the Titanic sank, though I do not think the two events were related. Possibly it was supposed that a life somewhat removed from the rigors of the road would better suit someone who later claimed to be delicate of health.

Whatever the reasons, Granny hung up her hawking basket and resigned herself to wifely duties at the wheelwrights yard.

She would often talk to my Mam of the time when her "old family," experienced itinerant knife grinders, were called upon by Joseph Rodgers of Sheffield, master cutlers in the north of the country, to sharpen knives at the factory. It was re-told that the monarch of the day had ordered a set of cutlery for the palace and that the master cutlers had scoured the area for someone who could hone the blades to the highest of standards. "We's is the dear peoples wot did grind for the Queen," was the Prices' proud boast. Then again, it may just have been a tale told to encourage customers to engage their services. At any rate my Mam believed it, and would often be found peering short-sightedly at the crests and trade marks on the blades of knives, from time to time exclaiming with genuine delight. "Look 'ere now Joseph Rodgers..." The rest of the comment would be cut short by my dad finishing the sentence "of ukin Sheffield, yes we all know, grinders to the "ukin Queen". Undaunted by this peremptory stealing of thunder. Mam still went to great pains to examine cutlery, all be it unobtrusively.

One relic of the cutlers tale was a set of apostle spoons made by the firm in question. They were housed in an ebony box lined with royal blue velvet. When company came to call, Mam would unveil the apostle spoons and proudly offer them round for use. At the end of the evening, she would scour the grass around the fire. "Wot hevers the dear woman a doing?" observers of this ritual would ask. "Oh pay no 'eed to 'er", my Dad would reply, "She'm

just a-rounding up the twelve hapostles don't you know."

Herbert the wheelwright and Ethel the hawker achieved some measure of marital harmony, though it never extended as far as bliss. Ethel pined for her family, though pride forced her to suffer in silence.

When wifely duties of cooking and washing were done she would roam the moors restlessly for hours "stalking the moon" and examining old stopping places for clues to it's inhabitants and their occupations. This left Herbert free to pursue a pint at the pub and the bar-maid who served it.

When Mam came along, one frosty December, Ethel decided Her Bert's public house shenanigans would come to an end. He was literally "Her Bert" and not to be shared with a puller of pints as well as husbands. When Granddad returned home, the family's goods and chattels had been loaded onto the new pram and his only option as he bounced of a locked door was to follow the determined Ethel until she lead him to his new place of lodgings.

Here the family set up a new home, this time with an outside earth closet and their own coal shed, not to mention a "hanging ground" for the drying of laundry. Ethel felt content enough to plant up a garden and gently scented the back yard with Lily of the Valley in remembrance of her sister Lily and her seven sons, Ethel's nephews. She also planted wallflowers in rich velvet Gypsy colours of maroon and gold. When Mam asked the significance of these blooms, she was told wistfully that it was to remind Ethel of her own mother who had planted her flower behind a wall. Ethel the walled flower. Herbert and Ethel stayed long enough at the new abode for Ethel to send her daughter to school. Herbert had no difficulty providing for his family, having now become foreman at the wheelwrights yard.

He also supplemented this with his efforts in the boxing booth, returning home bruised but victorious to have Ethel fuss round him administering with lint and salt water. Short and stocky, yet powerfully built, he was nippy on his feet which meant he could avoid the jabs of his larger and heavier sparring partners. Manual work at the yard kept him fit, added to which he had now been persuaded to join his wife on her country wanderings on the pretext of carrying his baby daughter, provided of course that they took place during daylight hours. Before long, he had grown fond of the exercise and enjoyed to see the pleasure it brought to Ethel.

In winter they would find a frozen pond or reservoir and he taught her how to skate, pulling baby along behind on a sledge he had knocked together at the yard. Things ticked along comfortably and Ethel seemed less restless. Never fully accepted by "Her Bert's" side of the family or even the neighbours and alienated from her own people, she doted on her daughter and they became very close.

Together, they fashioned clippy rugs, knitted blankets and crocheted lace and home became a brighter and more cheerful place.

When Mam was about in double years, Ethel gave birth to a second child. Sadly Mam's sibling did not survive and its loss tore at the very hearts of its parents. Ethel resumed her lone rangings of the moors and Herbert resumed his patronage of the pub, eventually finding comfort, as before in someone else's arms. There followed more "removes" to fresh lodgings. Mam was sent for music lessons and later to

learn to be a secretary. She was not destined for life in an office, however, because the second world war had broken out by now.

Following the loss of Ethel's second child, her health started to decline and Granddad decided it was time to bid farewell to the smoky industrial haunts of Yorkshire and head for pastures new where there were no old memories to haunt and an ample supply of fresh air.

Ethel and 'Her Bert' moved to Derbyshire and with the coming of World War II my Mam went to work in a munitions factory, followed by a stint of ambulance driving, at the end of which she was given a full driving license, by way of a thank you.

By the time the war had come to a welcome end, so had Ethel. She quietly and painfully passed away from "that complaint" at the tender age of 42. She had never recovered the loss of her child. After the funeral, Herbert, now free to concentrate on focusing his roving eye, lost all interest in what was on view. Finding the Ethel sized hole she left behind could not be filled, he ceased to try and went to join her at the earliest opportunity. He was rumoured to have died of a broken heart, but that may be at odds with the entry on his death certificate. When the war was finally over, Mam found herself parentless but not penniless, having inherited a reasonable amount following Granddad's demise.

4
A Wandering Star

Much has already been written about my Dad's childhood growing up with his parents Annie and Lally*, with their large family, of which my dad was the last, of their travels and his boyhood years. Two of my uncles had already joined up and gone to war. Some Gypsy boys avoided army service either by hiding away down the Fens or by changing their name or identity frequently. Another ruse employed was claiming to be unfit for service which involved claiming infirmity or worse still causing infirmity. It wasn't that they were cowards or even "conshies", just it didn't really seem to be their war, and many had large young families to support. My Dad simply had one Guinness too many and enrolled for service and the King's shilling whilst fully under the influence.

As well as Dad, two of his brothers joined up. Dad came home with four medals and a leg full of shrapnel. His brothers never came home at all. Dad rarely talked about his experiences, and we never thought to ask. Like my uncles, the past was buried. It was post war that my Mam and Dad met and after a very brief courtship sealed their union at the registry office in the district of Shardlow in Derbyshire. Afterwards, there was good old Travellers style bash at Bonsall Dingle then they sailed into married life, the recent past being laced with loss. Mam had returned to her roots and Dad had returned to Blighty. In those days, folks did more with less and before long they were "on their feet", even if their gait was wobbly.

By this time my Dad had a variety of Christian names that he could call upon and a not unsubstantial stock of surnames. Whenever he was asked, there would be an expectant pause while he struggled to remember exactly who he was supposed to be. In old age, he settled for Anthony George Joseph, a title which encompassed his favourite few. His death certificate, years later, was to state William, which was in fact his brother's name. Officially my dear old Dad is still with us.

My Dads signature tune, which he whistled quietly to himself in those peaceful yet rare moments of pure contentment, was sung by his hero, "gentleman" Jim Reeves — *I was born under a wandering star*. It perfectly summed up Dad's restless nature and low boredom threshold, his curiosity for what might lie round the next corner just out of sight. Reared on country music and cowboy films, it felt like Jim Reeves and John Wayne were part of the family.

My Dad wore suit trousers and a waistcoat, changing his shirt on alternate days. Never a wearer of braces, he preferred a thick leather belt with a brass buckle. He was known to warn that when times got hard, we would have to tighten our belts. I would anxiously count the holes at the end of his to see if it had been taken up a notch.

As there never seemed to be any variation, I always assumed financial disaster had been averted. Should he need a weapon with which to defend himself, he would wield the belt buckle, end outermost, to alarming effect. Not a wearer of jumpers or the other male fashion bastion cardigans, he never tired of his jacket and a silk *diklo** tied at his throat, in the style of the late Oliver Lee. I never saw him intoxicated and he was always home at night. Gambling held no fascination. Pigtail twist and snuff, however, were pleasures beyond measure and sacrifices were made to ensure their continued supply. Dad took solace and comfort from his pipe and in times of stress, the ritual of filling and lighting it and a few heady inhalations always took place with measured deliberation, while he marshalled his thoughts and came up with a reaction to whatever had arisen. This ritual could cause frustration to those spectators patiently waiting for some sort of response. With a dry sense of humour bordering on the arid, he could be good company.

A vast knowledge of wild plants and animals, as well as local knowledge of most English Counties in which he had travelled, meant he was able to find common ground with most people he conversed with. If called upon to sing, he could reasonably hold a tune though not fully grasp it. Playing the spoons with great gusto, as well as the bones, he joined in at many campfire music nights and accompanied Mam when she played the squeeze box or mouth organ. Neither Mam nor Dad were in the first flush of youth, nor even the second, so when I arrived, understandably, it took them by surprise but pleasingly so.

By the end of my first summer, they were ready for a shift and decided to pull to Warwickshire to get the horses re-shod before returning to the Vale for the start of the apple picking season in the autumn. Early one morning misty morning, as dawn broke, we were packed down and yoked up and on the road before the first skylark had sung. Dad liked ten miles under his belt before the day woke up. Before noon, we'd pull up "somewheres quiet" and let the worst of the traffic drive itself crazy.

The "nine to five slip on shoe brigade" were creatures of pity in Dad's eyes — their autonomous lifestyle of drudgery watching the clock held no charms for him. Not for them the mystery and uncertainty of freedom and independence, with only their own wits to rely on to provide for their families. The nearest any of them would get to the life we knew, would be a coach outing to the seaside in the summer and the relative peace and quiet of an allotment shed the rest of the year, tending a few sad cabbages and burning potato tops on a smokey bonfire.

By evening time, when the urbanites in their beige Morris Minors had quit the factory and returned to the comparative safety of a pre-fab or a city terracotta brick back to back, Dad was again ready to roll in the coolness of the evening, to his final resting place for the night. His thinking was that by the time he unyoked, the *local yokel muskra** would have put his bicycle to bed and be working his way through a Lancashire hot pot and waiting for the test card to make way for the evening's programmes on the black and white television set. That's if constabulary wages left enough over for an entertainment budget! In those days, there was no daytime television until evening came, just a still picture of a girl with an annoying smile posing in front of a blackboard. Once the time had come to draw the curtains and don the slippers, there were treats like *Dixon of Dock Green* and *Z Cars* in store, both involving cops and robbers and the cops always won.

In real life, the robbers sometimes won, especially on August 8th 1963 when the Post Office Express was ambushed at Cheddington, in Buckinghamshire and daringly relieved of £2.6 million. Much of the money was never recovered, neither was one of the instigators, Ronnie Arthur Biggs who escaped from Wandsworth Prison and spent 35 years in exile, much of it in Brazil. Country folk were largely impressed with the incident and widely wondered what they themselves would have done with the proceeds. Subsequently, the Post Master General issued a statement saying suggestions were being considered for tightening up security. You bet your pretty life they were. In those days a pound was worth a pound, even in "old money".

Travelling by back lanes and green tracks, Dad would "ride up" with a monarch's view over the hedges. His back braced against the chamfered waggon front, he would shade his eyes with a hand, the better to see about him. Hawthorn bushes, home to thrushes and finches, whistled and sang as we trundled along. With the road stretching a blue grey ribbon ahead and the pram stowed on the cratch we would whip up a brisk trot and with wheels humming and mane flying, hooves would reach a steady rhythm ringing on the road. These times Mam would smile sideways at Dad, one of those rare moments of which they were proud.

The troubles of the past were behind them and the challenges of the future hazily ahead.

"We'm a-mekin good time, Mrs Lady," Dad would offer.

"Now they motors has gone, yous own the road," Mam would comfort proudly.

Watching the expressions of joy on their faces intently staring ahead, I noticed Dad's worn trousers and down at heel boots, Mam's hands lined and rough, folded on her lap. I wondered at a happiness, that was clearly oblivious to these signs of poverty and lack. They considered themselves rich regardless of indications to the contrary. It was only some time later that I realised just how many different kinds of "rich" there are. Some riches hold subtle value, not immediately apparent and worth the more for being that way.

Beusale Common had been one of Dads stopping places for years. Grazed smooth as a mansion lawn it had sheltered seclusions of gorse and bramble which offered privacy, as well as a windbreak. How deliciously springy and scented the ancient turf was to a toddler's bare feet. Laced with vetches, trefoils and rabbit droppings, scars from previous Travellers fires were still visible. The last occupants had only recently departed if the buckled bike frame, brown beer bottles and "coronation" milk tins were anything to go by.

Had this been a ground my Dad had left, the bike would have gone in the scrap, the bottles would have been returned for the pennies paid as deposit and the milk tins hammered flat and stuffed down the nearest rabbit hole. This was good news for the environment but not necessarily for the rabbits.

In years to come, it was an anticipated source of pleasure to be first down from the waggon to "look for leavings" that might be of some use or at least give clues to who the previous occupants had been. Hair ribbons and sweet papers would show *chavvies** had stayed here, the labels on jam-jars giving hints as to their quality of *vittles** and therefore income.

Every camp seems to offer up an odd shoe, begging the question of what happened to its partner? It was hard to believe that there could be that many one legged people about.

With the waggon drawn in off the road, ease of practise had us set up in no time. As Mam set her out her little home, Dad set out with his dogs, adept at avoiding too much domestic responsibility.

With no watch, he would rely on the chiming of a distant church clock or the position of an ivory moon in a midnight sky to remind him it was time to head for home and the scent of wood smoke.

Approaching the camp silently, he would often pause, a restraining hand on his dogs head, soaking in the timeless scene before him, which doubtless invoked so many memories. The dusky silhouette etched on the sky line, waggon interior lit by the waxen yellow glow of an oil lamp punctuating the darkness.

His tired cob, still smelling of sweat, its back to the wind, resting one leg . A wary restless hound raising its head on hearing an approach. Dying embers casting a sepia glow. Simple, tantalising, timeless, satisfying.

After a few days on the common, we'd execute a short sharp shift into the blacksmith's yard at Hasleynob, or as it was called by villagers, the nob. These days, if a place is called "the smithy" the likelihood is that it is anything but. Instead it will have been "developed" which is a euphemism for destroyed. Tasteless white plastic double glazing will have been inserted round new windows which will blink out with surprise at a block paved driveway culminating in American style security gates. The property may be neighboured by "the old school house" which will also have suffered a similar fate. Neither horses nor children will frequent the area, probably all having been served with "asbos" at the request of the residents who feel they would detract from the country village atmosphere.

In the 1950s, a smithy was still a smithy and had a blacksmith, a church was still a church and had a parson who happened to live in a parsonage, rural England didn't go for new fangled labels.

Harry and Elsie Jackson, brother and sister, had a small aged black and white cottage next to the smithy where they had both been born decades earlier. The thatched roof, long due an overhaul, but not seeming to mind the wait, sported a fine crop of velvet moss — home to several sparrows who twittered and shitted on all who walked up to the front door. The brick path edged with hollyhocks and columbines in no particular order. With the sootied smithy to run and his sister to care for, Harry had given up on the taming of the weeds, contenting himself with scything pathways through the nettles and trumpet flowered bindweed which recklessly entwined damson and apple trees, as bent and

gnarled as Harry himself. It was along these scythed paths that Elsie would coax her veteran bantams back to their coop of an evening, before the fox saved her the trouble. The same shorn paths provided salking ground for the many cats which lived around the buildings. In the evenings, Elsie would meander her way to the washing line after ministrations with a mangle on faded cotton laundry. In later years. I would be left in the care of this fay, fragile, faded friend. Considering Elsie had no experience of childcare and little experience of life at all outside "the nob," she coped passably well with minding a tottering toddler. I was too young to speak and she too deaf to hear, so we communicated well enough with smiles and chattering and messages of the eyes, determinedly staggering behind her, trailing like a Macintosh belt through the avenues of pungent nettles, I would pursue her pinnied and slippered form to check on Dolly the cow in the buttercup meadow, or gaze contentedly while the kitchen range got leaded with "zebo", blackened and polished. Hours flew by, tick-tocked away by a grandfather clock, which also helped prop up the ceiling.

Clippie rugs got waved rather than shaken, cats lapped stale milk from mismatched saucers and red geraniums shed their petals and emitted a powerful odour in the low ceiling stone flagged kitchen.

Bereft of the alleged benefits of mains services, the cottagers got by as did Mam and Dad with oil lamps. Their "felicities" (facilities) extended to a pump which gushed forth sparking sweet well water to anyone willing to shake its hand and a lean-to privy at the rear of the property. Whitewashed absentmindedly by Harry, it boasted two round holes, side by side in the bleached wood ash seat of an earth closet. This was pre-WC era. Squares of newspaper, suspended from a rust nail offered reading or cleansing material or possibly both. It was bemusing to imagine brother and sister side by side, bum to bum, perusing the Beusale Bugle or the Methodist Times.

I found the cavernous prospect of the hole too daunting and had to content myself with peeing on the rhubarb instead. I had to content myself with passing on a pie of the same when it was offered for tea on Sundays.

Both devout and unquestioning believers, they lived their faith as surely as would have the apostles depicted on Mams spoons. Neither swore nor blasphemed, a tricky precedent for my Dad, who routinely indulged in both, at time reaching aficionado levels.

Elsie wore a cross over pinnie and a grey felt hat, severely impaled on her head with two pearl tipped pins. The only variance of this costume was the removal of the pinny for Sundays for the weekly exodus to chapel.

Neither wireless nor television intruded on their privacy though on balmy evenings when sunshine had warmed the cottage wall as it set, and the hollyhocks had cast their shadows, Elsie could sometimes be persuaded to softly play her little Welsh harp. With silver hair and a halo cast by lamp light, her angelic performance delighted listeners to the point of breath holding and a hallowed silence followed as the last tinklings faded away. Hers was a hard act to follow, those spiritually attuned had momentarily been transported audibly and visually to another realm and returned reluctantly to this earthly one.

Years later, electricity was installed by well meaning urbanites and a large black and white television positioned on the sideboard. Both were politely praised: "O, ain't that kind. 'Arry", then instantly ignored, the latter soon to be covered with a cloth of crocheted cotton to lessen it's impudent intrusion, and offer a better grip to the cats, who found the elevated vantage point of benefit when spotting wayward mice who happened through the ever open door on their way to the larder.

Soon the time would come to part again, we to wend our way towards apple picking time and they to sink into the smokey smell of smithy life and the cautious company of cats, as serene at our departure as they had been at our arrival. Timeless, gentle and enduring.

Unfettered by respect for the Jackson's propriety of speech, Dad would wend his way back to Worcestershire, keen to hone his cussing skills and make up for lost time. This pilgrimage was re-enacted many times, memory eclipses memory. I would have been only months old on my first visit.

Many years later, having journeyed up the country I came across a sign post for Beusale by accident, accompanied by my own daughter, herself the same age I had been when I made my first visit. Passing the common I was drawn back to "the nob" and the smithy with some trepidation, fearing the passing of so many years would have taken with it both my childhood friends.

As we grow, so places in our childhood begin to shrink and on rounding a bend in the lane I was struck at once by how tiny the blacksmiths cottage suddenly appeared. Nettles and friars balsam grew shoulder high and unscythed. The thatched roof had tufts of straw missing, moss and unruly grasses sprouted, reminiscent of a scarecrow's hat. Tiles were displaced on the old smithy roof, its disused door shut fast and bolstered with dry leaves. The garden gate hung loose. So sure was I by now that all inhabitants had long gone that I tried the door lightly expecting it to resist. The door swung open easily and the scent of geraniums and cats enveloped my baby. Sitting in the rocking chair was Elsie, smiling a benign and unsurprised welcome. "'Ello Ainlee, come on in". It was as if I had been there yesterday and arrived on cue as expected. Embers glowed in the range and Elsie's bright eyes shone with a placid smile.

Always of small frame she had now shrunk to childlike form. Now in her eighties, fragility belied inner strength. We drank tea together, she admiring the babe. Harry had passed away some years before, but Elsie had stayed on at the cottage, feeling per-

haps closer to him there than anywhere else. We talked of times past and shared our memories.

Deep in this rich and peaceful reverie we were tea spillingly startled when a portly tweeted gent in thick national health spectacles burst through the door, cracking his head with astonishing force on the low beam above. "Stop right there," he shouted, somewhat dizzied by the recent impact.

"Where?" enquired Elsie expressing no surprise at the unwarranted intrusion.

"Who the devil are you and what the blazes are you doing here"?

"It's only Ainlee, 'avin tea", replied Elsie.

Somewhat nonplussed by this introduction which clearly left him none the wiser with his quest, the portly gent affected a blustering retreat, ruefully rubbing the rapidly rising lump on his forehead.

"'E does that" informed Elsie by way of explanation, ignoring the episode as effectively as she had dismissed the intrusion of television and electric so many years before.

No further mention was made of our visitor. I assumed it was some neighbour having seen our vehicle parked in the lane, fearing for the old ladies safety, in these times of bogus callers and had come to investigate, therefore I was not vexed that she had a protector. Alternatively, it could have been a local lunatic with attention seeking tendencies.

As they say in the country, it all makes for wondering. We sat long into the evening, I wanting my daughter to imbibe the experience, for it was not likely to be repeated, my travels taking us to distant parts and my friends taking her to meet her maker.

When we finally parted, the old smithy was bathed in moonlight. I did not urge Elsie to bolt the door when I had departed, for the impression that she had a heavenly protector was very strong. Neither of us referred to the likelihood that this would be our final Farewell. Some things just can't be said, so laden would they be with emotion. Shortly afterwards the news reached me from other friends that Elsie had passed away. Elsie style, I ignored the information, preferring and drawing comfort from imagining her still, companioned by cats at 'the nob'.

5
Yesterday's Bread

Back on the road to Worcester, leaving Warwickshire behind at a rolling trot, there was an unspoken urgency as autumn whispered of its approach. Despite the sun's warmth, leaves floated downwards, bidding farewell to twigs they had adorned since spring. The cob's neck white with sweat, hooves and feathers flying as if sensing he was heading for home.

Momentarily distracted from the job in hand and knowing his horse's self steering skills, Dad surveyed the hedges and verges flying by. Bramble bushes laden with dark fruit on bowed stems suggested tempting pies and cordials. Dotted on the verge, cream crested mushrooms peeped through shortened grass invitingly waiting to be picked. On other days, we might have tarried to refresh our larder but orchards of cider and perry fruit awaited Mam and Dad's attention. Delay might mean our place usurped by other hopefuls keen to boost their income before the first frost of winter.

Dad was jolted from his punctuated pipe puffings, when the waggon bounced in and out of a drunken pot-hole in the road and Mam's meagre collection of "pots and crocks" rattled alarmingly in the waggons interior.

"Keep yer *yoks** on the road, dosey nose," Mam screeched, anxiously scrabbling inside to access the damage. "Me dear bits of things is all broke to bits, just look at 'em."

"Nowt a bit o' Bostick can't fix," offered Dad, "An think on the dustin' wot you'll save on", though privately wondering if the waggons wooden wheel had been damaged. That would take more than a dab of Bostick or anything else. It might mean our journey juddering to a splintering halt.

Realising that her rebukes were falling on stony ground and knowing that if she "kep' on" Dad was cussed enough to explore another pot hole on purpose, deviating course if needs be, she returned to her precarious position on the step board, soon admir-

ing for herself the curls of and tendrils of Travellers Joy unwinding from the bushes. Seeded heads reminiscent of tiny puffs of smoke.

"Watch the chimney gormless," she muttered as we shot underneath a particularly low oak branch which threatened to catch the stove pipe, wrenching it through the roof.

Pickfords certainly had the edge on Dad when it came to moving on this journey.

In later years as roads got busier with the increase in traffic, the accident rate increased. Some drivers couldn't get their foot off the accelerator and others couldn't locate the brake. For some unfortunates, the concept of three pedals alone presented just too much choice. Corners in particular proved a challenge for some road users. The co-ordination of steerage direction, foot work and gear change proving just too much for those who's previous mode of transport was so recently a bicycle.

In response to the accident rate, many of England's by-ways were mechanically mangled in the cause of road safety. Ancient hawthorn hedges handsomely hand laid and stock proof were ripped out by their roots with scant regard for the many years it had taken to grow them. Corners and bends were cleared of any impediment to the view.

To the "Toads of Toad Hall", who lusted for the power of speed, it was rural carnage that couldn't come soon enough. It offered the opportunity to go even faster with an unimpeded view — which adversely affected the accident rate even further as well as the character of English countryside. Folks with combustion engines thought nothing of going at forty miles an hour — manual dexterity permitting. Roads had to be made wider to facilitate a new craze — overtaking.

Frustrating indeed to be stuck behind a horse and waggon or tractor when there were all these "miles an hour" under the bonnet begging for expression.

Village landscapes started to change and our expeditions became tinged with trepidation.

Dad jumped down to walk the last few miles and lessen the cob's load. There would be no great unpacking tonight, just animals watered and a bread and cheese supper. At thirty miles a day, we would soon be pulled in the orchards and well away from prying eyes and the "tormentations" of traffic.

When an inviting side-road appeared, the main road was abandoned and we were just settling down for the night, when a bicycle bell sounded.

"'Oo is it?" queried Mam, fearing the *yokel muskra** might be calling.

"Marcia," the unseen cyclist replied.

"'Oo the uks Marcia?" enquired Dad who was on the down hill slope to his pillow.

"Get up and get rid," said Mam, who had already unbraided her hair, pre-slumber, and didn't want to be at home to any visitors, even ones called Marcia.

Reluctantly relinquishing his mattress, Dad peered out of the curtained window to disgruntedly appraise the unknown stranger.

Peering up hopefully was a be-curlered woman in her late twenties. Peroxided tresses of hair, bound tight round pink curlers were unattractively bound in place with a lime green nylon chiffon headscarf. Eyebrows had been severely pencilled in place and the effect of characterless lips, amplified by a smear of startling red lipstick. Her face gave the impression of having been snapped shut and the multitude of colours swam before Dads eyes, temporarily leaving him bereft of words. Conscious of his pillow flattened quiff and a graze of stubbly chin Dads confidence and *gorgia* talk had been left behind in bed.

"Wotcha want ?" he managed to mumble, wondering how best to get rid of the intrusion.

"Well I was wonderin', dus y' tell fortunes loik?" Marcia enquired, not rebuffed by his lack of charm, proffering a nail bitten hand in Dad's general direction.

Dad managed to avoid the protruding limb, responding with a rather lame "not tonight Josephine", before rapidly re-closing the curtains. There was a generous pause followed by a plaintive voice, "Me name's not Josephine, it's Marcia", followed eventually by the sounds of a bicycle being wobblingly ridden away. Dad checked the darkness and was satisfied to see the feeble light of the dynamo flickering away up the road.

"Dirty 'ore" muttered Mam, who had never even clapped eyes on our potential customer.

Next morning, we were on the road at first light and by noon were taking a hasty lunch of yesterday's bread and some cheese, partnered with piccalilli of a strength to take your breath away. The cob remained yoked in the shafts, but made the most of a well earned rest and a blow. By afternoon we had made such good time that the following day would see us at our appointed farm ahead of schedule. Arriving early for picking could sometimes be disconcerting for farmers who only wanted workers while the crop was being harvested.

Therefore it was with some misgivings that we arrived at the orchards at Upton-Upon-Severn. Mam had just unpacked the waggon and Dad lit the fire, when the farmer appeared through a distant gateway making purposefully in our direction. Although his approach had been noted, we continued as if not to have noticed, wondering what his reaction would be.

With a battered hat shading his eyes, it was hard to determine any facial expression that might give a clue as to the degree of welcome we might expect to receive. He reached us with long strides, corduroy trousers embracing long legs thrust deep into

Wellingtons. A worn khaki shirt and tweed jacket gave an appearance that belied this gentleman farmer's true financial standing, being in fact a major landowner in the area and supplier of cider fruit to the industry, Bulmer's cider.

Dad greeted him with an "evening Boss" tactically avoiding eye contact for as long as possible and offering a subservient approach which would not have come to him naturally.

"A fine evening, yes indeed" came the reply.

This left the ball firmly back in Dad's court again.

"We's made better time 'an what we's hexpected, the 'oss being so fit as wot 'e is."

Dad glanced sideways as the ball made a return journey. Mam shuffled and tried not to hold her breath, uncertain whether to carry on unpacking which might appear presumptuous or re-pack which might appear defeatist.

"I noticed he looked in good condition" the farmer parried back.

Dad started pocket-patting, the forerunner to the pipe priming routine. He subscribed to the old maxim 'If in doubt get the old *swegler** out'. An expert in long pauses and strategic silences, we all watched pig-tail twist being cut on the palm of his hand then rubbed to a useable consistency with his finger tips.

Either the landowner cracked first or he fancied getting home for his supper. Either way, he was first to comment that the crop wasn't quite ready to be picked anyway because a labourer earmarked to prepare the pickers sacks and baskets etc had been called away to other duties, setting them further behind schedule.

"I'd be 'appy to step into the bleach if it'd 'elp yous out," Dad offered, concealing his eagerness from his voice.

"Yes indeed" said the farmer, pushing his hat back from his head, revealing twinkling eyes and the suggestion of a smile. "I'll bid you goodnight and see you in the morning." With this he touched his hat to Mam who exhaled with relief like a rapidly deflating balloon.

Dressed in a fleecy siren-suit all-in-one, I was washed and put to bed, the end of another long and exciting day. Another day another deal, as Mam would say.

The next morning was the first of many that fell into a comfortable routine. Up early, Mam would fly through her domestic routine and following the obligatory "lick and promise" we would be out enjoying the autumnal mist disappearing and sun breaking through to deliver "St. Luke's little summer" as Mam called it, or what Dad referred to as "the back end".

Armed with a thermos flask and bacon butties, we would head for the orchards and deposit our repast in its basket below the broad trunk of an apple tree.

There were Conference pears to pick, dappled green eating pears, firm to the touch and even firmer to the teeth. These were packed away in wooden bushel boxes prior to be collected by tractor and despatched for market, ripening on route.

Early eating apples came next, varieties like Worcester Permain, Discovery, and the older Cox's Orange Pippin which rattled when it was ripe as the pips vibrated against their casing. A highly aromatic fruit, juicy and sweet, capable of retaining its cheerful good looks well into maturity like a graceful pensioner, with only a slight wrinkling of the skin!

In these ancient orchards, recipients of diligent husbandry, age old varieties flourished. Bran Rose, Cherry Norman, Dymock Red, Sweet Splash and Old Bromley. Rich names that rolled off the tongue, soon to be lost from general usage. Apples untampered with by people with ideas of genetic modification and the "dwarfing" of trees which produced fruit diminished in flavour also. Cider has been around since before 900BC. In Roman times, traces of cider apples have been found as far apart as Bermondsey and Doncaster. Traditionally, cider was made of one third each of sweet, bitter sweet and sharp apples, with the levels of tannin and acidity varying in each, the precise blending of the drink being part of the art of the master cider maker.

Once the early eating apples and pears had been boxed, we moved onto cider fruit proper, most of which had intimated its ripeness for harvest by relinquishing its hold on the supporting twig and descending with a satisfying thud on the ground below, (or the head of a picker) displaying themselves like doyleys round the trunks. We would work until lunch time, propping pungently scented hessian sacks against the trees. Out would come butties and flask for refreshment, hastily eaten astride a sack.

In the afternoon, my nap in a pram, gazing upwards to the sky, the silhouette of the dark branches above.

In later years, when sacks had been stacked on a corrugated iron floored trailer, I inadvertently cleared the orchard of pickers. On one particularly warm day, idle curiosity drew a small child to observe sacks left overnight on a conveyance. Noticing a trickle of amber liquid forming a riverlet along the channel, I enterprisingly stuck a jam-jar underneath to collect the contents. The resultant clear sparking contents resembled apple juice with its heady, pleasing flavour. It proved a popular source of refreshment to the other pickers present, and demand was in danger of exceeding supply requiring much bouncing on the sacks of fruit to produce more liquor. Having done the rounds once to great adulation the process was repeated for the rest of the afternoon. Long draughts of free refreshment were enjoyed by all participants.

During the night, the yeast content in the over-ripe fruit proceeded to ferment, albeit in the stomach of the recently refreshed. The following day, "Bod" the gentleman farmer arrived to orchards deserted of workers. Reports of "colly-wobbles', stomach cramps and downright diarrhoea were rife. We made a fine piecework profit that week being the "last men standing" — the rest relegated to racing to the privy, wrenching clumps of "Izal medicated" (now wash your hands please) to staunch the flow.

Cider picking fell into its own routine. With camp set up in the orchard, we were literally "on the job". Dad was offered milk from the dairy by Noel, (obviously once a Christmas born babe) the cowman, and honey from the hive. Potatoes were available from a nearby straw covered clamp. In real terms he had the run of a very extensive estate at no cost whatever to his pocket. In exchange, on Saturday nights, the farmer and his wife, who happened to be a local magistrate, brought parties of "hunt friends" etc to "meet the Romanies." Around a roaring fire, Mam played the accordion and Dad rattled out rhythm on "the bones". I step-danced on an

upturned beer tray and afterwards passed round a hat for shillings and hopefully half crowns to an audience ensconced on straw bales slurping cider. With our visitors well on the journey to inebriation, Mam told fortunes, for a consideration in the waggon, whilst Dad took lucrative orders for pegs and line props. As we neared Christmas, he added Holly and Mistletoe to his stock list. Life was sweet and living made very easy! When the evening was over and cider casks empty our rural revellers rebounded off trees on their journey though the orchard back to the farm. Many's the cow-pat inadvertently trodden in on their wavering journey back to their cars.

A few got a fair kick off the newly installed electric fence as well — all adding to the general experience. Afterwards, as flames danced on embers and the night relaxed into a sigh, we'd walk up the hill with Dads long dogs, to view the twinkling lights of Malvern away in the distance and I'd swing on the five bared gate for a while, knowing "Bod" was long abed thanks to a generous dose of Bulmers. Dad would cup his hands and call to the owls who dutifully hooted in reply and we too would head home to bed, fulfilled and content.

6
A Child
of the Wild

As frosts increased and pheasants were spotted stepping through ice encrusted grass, the numbers of pickers lessened. Finger numbing work which invited chilblains and "chaps" was relinquished in favour of indoor work as far removed from the elements as possible. We worked orchards so far "inland" that we'd to walk to them along mud rutted tracks, sometimes across many fields. Without the company of other Travellers, Mam and Dad doggedly picked on, often in silence. Bored by the quietness I would wander to explore.

In view of the "grey muddy", the river Severn, near Ripley, there was a high banked moss path called Donkey Lane. Bordered by sharp holly bushes and cheerful pink and orange "spindle" wood, its steep mossy banks were studded with lacy ferns. The holly bushes met overhead, making it a darkened, leaf-floored tunnel. According to the *Domesday Book*, in ancient times, panniered donkeys had travelled to the edge of the river with vast quantities of salt obtained from the brine springs at Droitwich. Once at the lapping river's edge, the precious cargo of 'worth its salt' fame was ferried across the water or "barged away to Brum".

Enchanting to a child as Donkey Lane was, it held unfathomable terrors to me. On the one side of the hedge was the extensive estate of Ryalls Court, then owned by the Surman family on whose ground we "stopped". On the other side was a neighbouring farm owned by the Goodwin family, a favourite haunt of Dad's for "mangold pulling". Betwixt the two properties and half way down Donkey Lane were the sooted gables of a black and white cottage. The inhabitants and their children had tragically been victims of a fire caused by a candle which caught hold of the thatch. Too far from a serviceable road for an engine to attend and convenienced only by a pump in the yard, the family had perished, the parents also, in their vain attempts to rescue their offspring, died, hearing their children's screams.

Often in the leafed lane, I would catch glimpses of smocked youngsters laughing and waving in the distance, inviting me to join in their games and play. Childrens spirits, drawn to a child, beckoning entreatingly. Smiling faces framed with ringlets and curls, a boy, short trousered and booted.

I never ventured into the lane at dusk, or the cottage ruins if I was alone. When Dad was nearby holly gathering, brave and emboldened I'd scramble down the bank to examine charred embers and what remained of the beams and an iron range, still resident in the gable end. Rusted relics of domestic utensils, vessels and pots were buried under ashes and leaves. Tin soldiers and scared faced porceline dolls kept each other desolate company. Had these vessels been frantically used to no avail to quench the flames? How futile and desperate the families plight.

Near the edge of Donkey Lane, reachable only by foot, was the Day House, two red brick cottages of great age with tangled unkempt gardens and darkened damson trees.

One side of the Day House was empty. The other was inhabited by an old lady called Ivy Williams. I called her Miss Iggy and was both fascinated and afraid by the fact that she talked to herself. Doubtless the extremes of loneliness and isolation that she experienced had affected her. Roaming many miles collecting fire sticks and searching for her cats, she had inverted into a world entirely of her own, from which the rest of the universe revolved around her apparently unnoticed.

Behind her cobweb windowed cottage, which appeared as unkempt as its owner, the lush river meadows grew verdant and fresh. The Severn flowed placidly along, punctuated periodically with lazy barges and light pleasure craft, unless it was time for the Severn Bore, a tidal wave surge that enraged and roared along the rivers course, taking with it tufts of bank and tree trunks as trophies, proof of its potent power. Awesome to watch, especially if rains had been heavy and flood water had boosted the swell. At these times, drowned beasts, sheep and cows would float past bloated with stomach gas, legs upward and stiffened. Little creosoted fisherman's shacks floated from foundations, cruised into sight, white edged windows hanging open, gingham curtains flapping, pent roof offering a perch for tired seagulls.

We never camped near the river, she being too much of a capricious lady to be trusted to know her place. Too risky, our little wooden waggons might take to the water at will or tethered horses be put in danger. I found the river, like many things, fearful yet fascinating. Then again, I lived in a world where according to Mam, Dad and "me Granny", terror lurked hopefully round every corner. We were deluged with danger.

Gorgias were to be avoided at all costs, a very risky species. Other Travellers had to be treated with caution in case I inadvertently divulged information which "like a bride's drawers" was best left unrevealed. Strangers, farm labourers and "colliers" (nothing to do with coal) were to be treated with the same civility accorded to aliens.

Ponds and wells held risks never to be tampered with and these warnings were intended to keep a little child of the wild wary when exploring. On encountering a stranger, therefore, it became expedient to hide in the grasses or run away, a habit still present today.

At the end of a day in the orchards, we'd wander wearily home, the waggon a welcome landmark willing us back. On hearing voices, dogs barked in excitement and anticipation. Horses raised their heads enquiringly, stock still, ears pricked. We'd collect hedge sticks over the last few yards, maybe an aged birds nest, dry moss lined to ease our fire's ignition. The wood ash from the mornings fire powdery, fine and white. Often Dad would "put a stump on" and bank up the dry embers so that the "heart" stayed in all day, idly easing smoke. When required, the stump rolled back, twigs scattered, then fanned to a flame. Dropping on one knee Dad blew encouragingly, bowing and puffing to the 'fire dragon' 'til flames danced to life. He made a good fire, brazen brisk and business like. Breathing life into his fire imbued him with fresh energy, each exhaled breath releasing weariness, 'til fatigue had been cast off like an old coat, With his dogs now loose and a bucket slung over his shoulder, it would be his time to saunter off whistling and to water his horse in both senses of the phrase. He privately favoured the idea that land work was best reserved for fools and horses.

Mam embraced her evening routine with practised grace. With a fresh pinny on and a quick wash down, she'd be peeling potatoes

deftly with the aid of a cut down kitchen knife, finely honed to cut throat sharpness. Quartering the pealed pearls in her palm, they plopped promisingly into her black pot just as water approached the boil. With lid capping the pan at a dislocated tilt, enough steam was allowed to escape, to prevent boiling over, which in turn would douse the flames.

Apple picking time, we had bushel box seats and other improvisations depending on our flow of visitors. Oil drums and milk crates got called to duty as well as upturned buckets. Many of the men would sit as their forefathers had, crouched on their heels or even propped on one elbow lying side downwards on one hip, reverently leaving the proper seats for the women, especially those nursing children or of advanced years.

Romany folk prefer to partake of food in private, so the race was on to be fed and fortified before fresh company arrived. While supper simmered and rich aromas arose with appetites to match, Mam shook mats and 'wiped round a bit' with a flourish and pride inherited from Granny Ethel. Her waggon was her palace.

Tartan blankets in cheering checks of red and yellow spread with velvet cushions. Brocade curtains curtailed draughts, providing privacy. Fripperies of lace lightened and lifted the interior. On the small table, a nickel champagne cooler embraced a clutch of cutlery (mostly claiming to be "EPNS') and Dads briar wood pipe, mouth piece marked from repeated clenching between his teeth. A hurricane lamp, paraffin primed stood ready to be wick trimmed and lit. Likewise a half burned candle in blue enamel holder.

With bed shaken down and floor swept, Mam's chores were nearly done. On cold evenings, Mam would call into service an obliging if not robust Beatrice stove that ran on oil. Double burnered in dapple grey enamel it could grudgingly be coaxed to boil a kettle with reasonable speed if the weather was very bad. Other than that, mam did everything that she needed to do on her outside stick fire. In winter, snow flakes rested on her head and shoulders, seeming to dust her form like icing sugar. Rougish smoke prompted her to sigh in despair or take evasive action. If the wind was changeable this action resembled a war dance. Dad would mutter to himself woefully, "I'd a bin 'appy wi' a bit of old bread and some cheese."

With *vittles** eaten at speed and pots wiped clean, the evening enveloped. By late autumn, darkness encroached the daylight greedily. Dad would build up the fire till it illuminated the entire camp. The seasons determined my bed time — in autumn, it got earlier and earlier. Lying in bed I would listen to the wild winds tearing through the trees, buffeting the waggon sides with force full gusts and causing it to rock and roll on its underworks. Sometimes it would be necessary to alter its position so the wind hit the back of the waggon instead of the sides, or to drive wooden stakes deep into the ground, roped to the chassis to lower the risk of overturning.

On stormy nights, rain would trickle down the chimney pipe and drum on the roof like a thousand dancing fairies with clogs on. We rarely had the waggon doors closed at night time so I could lie awake and watch the stars in a deep blue frost filled sky or see the moonlight cast deep shadows, natures flood light in the sky.

Gypsy time is governed by neither clock nor convention, rather, by instinct and inspiration. Some evenings, we would just have retired for the night when a volley of sharp barks would warn of visitors approach. The arrival of a van would be heralded by hoots on the horn and hails of, "Is ye abed yet?" to which Dad shouted "NO" and meant YES! While he jumped down to "slow 'em up a bit", Mam would re-pin her hair and we would all throw coats on. These delicious diversions from dream time were always an unexpected source of excitement. While more wood was thrown on the fire, often encouraged by a splash of paraffin, Mam would rinse out the tea-pot and try to find as many mismatched cups as she had visitors.

"Only iffen you's am makin' it, don't you know."

"Well gooo on then, 'arf a cup won't 'urt."

"Don't want to put yous to no trouble mind."

Women congregated to one area and men to another, both hotbeds of witty banter in the firelight.

"An' they *muskras** come to us in an old 'trol car an sez to we as they'd go over us with a fine toothbrush till they fun' the hevidence," old Ishmael could be heard explaining, spitting indiscriminately to emphasise his point.

"Fun" the hevedence?... plant it more like! But we's is too sharp, my brother, for the likes of they," Liberty warmed to the subject.

"Most I's ever *chored** is a *choomia** off a pretty *rackli** but they'd try to find summik to make it wuth their while." Young Shady was a likeable lad with the makings of a Cliff Richard hair cut and more than his fair share of affability and good humour.

Old Ishmael ignored the attempt at stealing his thunder, adjusting his black velour hat with a heavily ringed hand to focus attention and play for time. Ever the showman, like Dad, he knew the power of the pause. "It's as true as wot I is sut 'ere, bebby die iffen it ain't, on me dear mothers grave, swear on the holy blessed bible, they's is out to get we, one way or another." Young Shady affably conceded to his elder. There is still due respect accorded to age and experience in the Romany community, a trait that settled society could benefit well from emulating, and a virtue most heartening to observe.

The firelight illuminated character-full faces, prematurely aged like leather lacking linseed, by the rigors of a life lived almost entirely out of doors and the stress caused by the effort to survive in an otherwise hostile society. While Men discoursed on all subjects male, the women at a respectful distance tugged their skirts to cover crossed ankles and pinned knees closely together to avoid the shame or *ladging** of public censure. This code of conduct was an unspoken rule of how "the right sort of travelling woman" deported themselves in public or mixed company, modesty being a virtue and mystery being a by-product. In an era of widely accepted sexual freedom, such custom seems quaintly sweet.

As my granny was wont to quote, "Might as well show your arse as your ankle", if too much flesh was inadvertently exposed.

"An' I am a-telling you's, proper blousy piece an no mistake, no better 'an it should be an no mistake..."

"That'll be a 'andful when it grows up, you mark my words ifen it ain't."

"Theres no knowin' what colour *chivvy** it'll bring home, an' I might as well say it as think it."

"Iffen it was mine, it'd be fitted with a charity belt."

"You's couldn't find a 'otter 'ole in the noon day sun in Calcutta an what you's got there."

As babes in arms were cuddled and rocked to sleep wrapped in old coats or blankets the moon rose in a clear night sky. Conversation rose and fell until propriety indicated that it was time for our visitors to depart. With much goodwill and affability, not knowing when fate would reunite, our friends repacked themselves in the van in a tangle of arms and legs. Dad obligingly tied the back doors shut with a length of binder twine, otherwise known as 'farmer's friend'. After a few experimental turns of the ignition, it juddered away down the track, hooting and tooting till disappearing from view.

When the very last of the filled apple sacks had been loaded on the trailer, there was a finality about the process that brought the curtain down on another season. The flattened grass between the shafts, turned muddy in places showed how long we had been in one place. Tell tale rust on the iron shod waggon wheels confirmed the fact. Dad honoured his early holly orders, gathering it in sacks from Donkey Lane, berried and shiny, bunched with string. Likewise the mistletoe, olive green and sticky of stem. This poisonous parasitical plant grows high in the branches of old trees, its most popular host being the apple tree. The druids believed this sacred plant offered protection from evil, whilst others declared it a symbol of aphrodisiac fertility and love, hence its popularity as a kissing bough. In Brittany, they believed our Lords cross was made of mistletoe wood, but as Dad said, "It ud 'av 'ad to be a bloody big clump".

In the 1950s, most of the mistletoe was harvested in the Midlands, the "three counties" of Worcestershire, Herefordshire and Gloucester being prime contributors, with mistletoe auctions being held annually at the market town of Tenbury Wells during November and December. Before moving to our wintering *atchin tan** there were preparations to be made. Mam went through the waggon to discard any possessions amassed during our sedentary cider season in those days when the seasons seemed more clearly defined, summer clothes were packed away in favour of winter woollies and itchy tweeds. Dad donned the turned down wellies and a pair of long johns and Mam got her boots out and an extra petticoat. Little girls could be seen in trousers, with a tartan skirt on top to emphasise femininity, certainly a lot of layers to contend with. Balaclavas and pixie hoods were donned by those unconscious of fashion. As the days went by, the fire consumed much of our excess — choices had to be made — either, or. If the chooser agonised too long, Dad consigned both to the fire and the ditherer was left with neither. This fostered a habit of snap decision making with the option of repenting at leisure. The 'use it or lose it" policy simplified life no end. On the final day bushel boxes would be hidden in a hedge for next year and the disembowelled radiogram (walnut veneer) that had served as a dog box joined the pyre, leaving its homeless occupant to slink shivering and uncertain into the hedge bottom.

A last trip to Upton to stock up with essentials for the journey and treats from Dad's final pay packet! "Amphlets" the newsagents provided an *Exchange & Mart* and boxed snuff for Dad, and a *Woman's Own* for Mam. The Epicure, with its white coated assistant, smelling strongly of gorgonzola, served packages of black pudding and polony, wrapped in greaseproof paper. He was also a stockist of Eiffel Tower lemonade crystals, and I was a willing customer.

Mr Clarke, the butcher, supplied Mam's tripe order — unfortunately so for those not considering themselves to be "connie sewers". Our route home took us package-laden past Miss Payne's sweetshop. A low doored lop-sided black and white timbered building of great age, matched only by its bent back proprietor who appeared of even greater years. The polished mahogany counter had for years separated customers from sweets. Smelling strongly of peppermints, there was an array of delights to entice those clutching large 1d's, while Miss Payne laboriously shuffled an approach. So great was her curvature, that with chin clamped to chest, direct eye contact with smaller customers behind the counter was near impossible. Her degree of deafness made the order inaudible as well.

Large black lidded glass jars with screw tops hosted rainbow drops droolingly suckable, gum defying liquorice filled comfits, lemon sherbets, spangles and chocolate limes. Miss Payne would indicate each contained confection in turn with an arthritically miss shaped forefinger, until eager nods of assent confirmed she had reached the desired destination. Another long and wheezing pause whilst she shuffled to the scales, then some "tip it and shake" till the quarter pound was reached. The silver scale pan slithered its sugary contents into a cone shaped white bag. So breath-holdingly slow was the whole operation that pennies had grown warm and sweaty in chubby fingers by the time the moment of transaction actually took place. Heading back over the swirling waters of the river, dawdle footed for home we bid a silent farewell to faces and friends, fields and fences which we would revisit until the following year.

Mam and Dad effected a lavender dawn departure, up and away while the farm lay sleeping, revelling in the mystery of here today and gone tomorrow, nurturing ingrained intrigue. By now, the cob's coats had thickened like teddy bears, for winter, nature's preferred protection from biting winds and flurries of snow. Not now the leisurely rumble on rustic by-ways but a journey chilled with intention. With heads down and collars up, walking along-side our home was the preferred option just to keep warm, barely the objects of envy. While watery sunlight leaked through leaden skies and folks intent on their own concerns paid scant attention to our passing, Mam's lips remained immobile as her mind enquired "how much further..." The frost had barely lifted all day, pot hole puddles fringed black and white, cracked ice cob-web spread splintered under foot. A white wood sign post welcomingly predicted *Grafton Flyford 2 miles*. Steadily the waggon cob leaned

into the collar, eager as well to be off the road before dark. Passing a lone leafless poplar tree, Dad veered down a high verged rutted track choosing a flatter patch near a gateway to swing in wide near the hedge.

Numb-fingered, Dad sporting a dew-drop, they fumbled to unbuckle the harness prior to unyoking. Despite the cold, once plugged out on the tether the cob lowered himself to roll, practised in the art of not entangling in the chain. Rising, he shook himself bodily before exploring the hedge bottom to draw wisps of grass with whiskered lips.

"'E 'm earned a truss 'o 'ay an' some oats", remarked Dad proudly, relieved to "'av" a-got wur we'm agoing".

Chilled, chastened and charitable, it was time for a dish of tea boiled on the Beatrice stove and an early visit to the blanket show.

7
The White
Grit Road

The track down which we had pulled led at one end to Bob Cowley's farm and at the other to Grafton Flyford. Grafton Flyford is part of the old English trio of villages known collectively as the Flyfords — Grafton Flyford, Flyford Flavel and the charmingly named North Piddle, locally the butt of much "hey diddle diddle" humour. Grafton Flyford had adeptly avoided authorities" general interference, its existence having changed little since the *Enclosures Act* passed on the village in 1780. Now owned by George Wiliam, Earl of Coventry, it proudly boasted 162 woods and plantations, Grafton Woods in the south east being renowned for the finest cover for foxes in the county. They were the best primrose and bluebell woods as well. Progress of sorts had grudgingly run to a metalled road being laid and the installation of a telephone Box. One or two inhabitants had electricity and those on the "high street" —which was the only street — had mains water. Enthusiasm for modernisation had rapidly wained before mains sewerage was imposed, so disposal methods fell into two camps, the privy based "bucket and chuck it" brigade and the "sceptic tank," let's dig a gully to the ditch, school of sanitation. The former had the edge on the latter especially in high summer when "the ditch ran dry and the stench got high".

Success at the horticultural shows was testament to the recycling ingenuity of some gardeners. Waste not want not often meant they won "turd prize".

Although Mam and Dad retired early on that first night, rising meant a frosty fire blazing and a degree of domestic activity that gave rise to the impression that we had been there for weeks. With mats shaken, bedding put to air on a nearby gate and the waggon scrubbed and sparkling, Mam felt she had made in-roads into the day. Tutored by Granny Ethel, she had been strictly schooled in the practise of the "famous five" "sweep your hearth, pickup your bed, wash your pots, shake your rugs and sweep the floor. Likewise by Grandad Lally, Dad had picked up the habits of "shift the 'osses, feed your *juks**, light your *yog**, *praster** for *pani** and earn your bread money". How early in life are the necessary habits to ensure survival instilled.

Often, our family would open its arms to embrace the arrival of others. Uncle Norris, "Nos Nos," would arrive from nowhere unannounced. Shod in turned-down Wellingtons, he could turn his hand to anything and was a dab hand at peg and basket making in particular. Well able to tackle scissor grinding and that of knives, he was a useful addition to the family, usually leaving Mam's food hamper fuller when he went than when he arrived. Taking harsh weather with indifference and well sculptured by the hammer and chisel of adversity in all its many hues, he arrived that morning with a financial status by no means the subject of envy. He didn't just take each day as it came, always a chancer, he played it by the hour. Never having owned a key or a clock, he dismissed most of life's crisis's as storming a tea-cup insisting every avenue available had been explored and he'd left "no tone unsturned".

Mam surveyed the silhouette of leafless elm trees gracing the horizon, counting the crows nests to which they played host. Exactly how much diluting would the stew pot need to extend its contents to feed another mouth? Still, the company was welcome and Dad and Uncle Norris set to, to earn enough shillings to ensure we all benefited from "a damn good Christmas".

Withy stalks, stripped white and bound bright with tin, spun off peg knives with the practised ease of a production line. We had not realised then that this would be the last generation in a long line of ancestors to make their money this way. Bundles of hazel sticks miraculously transformed into criss-cross baskets, which Mam attractively embellished with ivy twisted round the handle and teasels and spindle wood packed tight in moss. On occasions, Dad would shave wooden flowers, dye dipped so she could 'spin 'em out in no-time' when calling at the doors. Holly and candles could be added to ring the changes. Lined up on the step board, prior to hawking, they made a pleasing sight and I was proud to see what they had been able to produce, eeked as it was from the hedgerow and supplimented with a bit of creative ingenuity.

Early next morning, while Dad used the mountain of peg shavings to light the fire, Mam rounded up some more girls as "carriers', tied on a clean pinnie and booted and brisk we set out for a day's hawking round the doors.

The white grit road that ran through the High Street — which was the only street — was occasionally dotted with habitations, small hiccups of domesticity in an otherwise rural landscape. The first of these was the home of Nellie Pugh and her husband Smiler — an unlikely name, because he wasn't one. Nellie, a native of Pontypridd had come to work on a nearby farm in the second world war as a land girl. By the time the war had finished, Smiler had seeped his way into her affections, as surely as the local marl clay had seeped into her boots. He encroached on her earnings quite effectively as well, and this Welsh girl with a warm heart had soon succumbed to subbing his cider. Nellie's industrious nature made up for his work shy apathy.

They set up home in a corner of the pear orchard in a cornflower blue caravan, accessed by a two-plank footbridge, over a slow moving ditch, home to frogs and fast growing watercress. The corn-flower blue theme had extended to the homemade picket gate set in a neatly clipped privet hedge. At the side of the gate, also recessed into the foliage, was a white enamel bin with matching lid and the word BREAD enamelled on it. This was the repository for deliveries of milk, post and newspapers — Smiler being a bit of a *Daily Mail* man. Few envied Nellie her Daily Male and he was considered to be "overly greasy" and sly in a style no-one could quite put their finger on. This said, they both seemed to rub along with a measure of happiness. In those days, couples embarking on matrimony had made their bed and it was deemed necessary by most that they lie on it, whether it resulted in sweet dreams or not was another matter. Mam made a point of avoiding "calling" when Smiler was at home but with Nellie's bike clearly visible, it meant she at least was at home. Mam bid two of her "carriers" Athaliah and Amherdine to wait outside on the verge, guarding her "stock". "Don't want to crowd the dear woman do we now?"

Nellie appeared at a gingham-curtained caravan window and thrust forward a curlered head embraced in a headscarf and knot-ted at the front. "Awwwgh now, if it isn't yourself back now" she sang out in her clear Welsh trill, "Haven't I just been saying to Smiler now how its coming to "ewer" time of "yur"'. Mam and Nellie embroiled in their reunion were oblivious to the girls fidg-eting impatiently from one stockinged foot to another. Not until two baskets and some pegs were sold did Mam appear to remem-ber her assistants and only then, so they could carry the string of onions and a turnip she had managed to be gifted.

Once out of sight, any cadgings were hidden from view under my blankets in the pram, it was good hawking practice to look as needy and unfortunate as possible as a way of extracting sympa-thy. Bidding a grateful goodbye to our most recent benefactor Nellie, we headed off towards the village as briskly as burdens would allow, Mam admonishing Athalia and Amherdine "not to swing "em else your bits will fall out", with regard to the decora-tive baskets.

After a few more cottages and a few more sales we came upon the newest and latest development in Grafton, a bungalow, belonging to another woman, possibly also of Welsh origin Mrs Powell. Her husband, Mr Powell was bedridden (a phrase conjour-

ing mental images of a largely unsavoury nature) hence the bungalow. I would gurgle "Pow Pows blingo" with glee, knowing what a very affable and accommodating woman his wife was. Mam's tentative knock at the door resulted in a call of "hang on a minute I'm not as fast as I used to be" from within, followed by the shuffling sound of slippered feet on tiles. The door was opened at last to reveal a woman past middle age with grey hair constricted in a whispy bun, displaying merry eyes and a toothless grin residing above generouse layers of chins. A cross over pinnie helped disguise the lack of any support garment in the vicinity of her vast bosom. Bare legs were clad in stockings which had resigned any pretence of vertical positioning and comfortably encircled thick legs thrust into check slippers. "Well I never me dears, and it's pleased I am to be seeing you back round these parts." She patted Mam's forearm and beamed at the little deputation assembled on her door step " I was saying I needed more of your husband's pegs, I'm sure nothing holds a blanket on the line like one of his pegs".

It was rumoured that, during a particularly boisterous laundry session, she had accidently fed through the rollers a portion of her pendulous busom, hence Dad and Uncle Norris called her Mangled Tit when in their own company. Jiggling the pram handle absent mindedly, she distributed twists of barley sugar to us all and producing a snap clasp leather purse extracted a ten shilling note and some silver to pay for her purchases. "Now I know you're back down the lane I'll call by with some bits I've put by," she promised, slipping a fruit cake and jam tarts in Mams basket. With cheery waves we again repaired to the lane to decant to the privacy of the pram. Lightened by a lessening in load and in high spirits with our good fortune and sales performance, Mam pressed on to her next port of call.

Stepping up a cinder path to a low roofed timber cottage she whispered, "Miss Osbourne lives here, behave yourselves". The female that answered our knock was clearly a spinster and exuded a forlorn air of melancholy that gave rise to Mam "betting she lost her young man in the war an' never got over it". Her expression and sad eyes suggested a whole symphony of losses from which she had never quite rallied. What a stark contrast to "Pow Pow Mangle Tit", our last customer who's placid enjoyment of life was so magnetically evident those close, could bask in her aura of well being, even if she did smell slightly of pee. After much anxious cardigan clutching Mam's quarry capitulated and grudgingly conceded to "just a dozen then"

"It'll bring you luck Miss" Mam encouraged, smiling to engage reciprocation, though without success.

Reversing the way we had come, all felt slightly chastened at the individual we had beheld, as if a cloud had passed over the sun.

At the next door, a young woman in a tabard apron and shockingly short, almost knee length woollen skirt, wrenched open the door surveying us with a suspicious stare and a "Yais?". Mam showed the last of her baskets and the cream coloured soldiers of pegs lining her basket. Despite much wheedling and cajoling, the woman still remained unmoved, managing to utter a monosyllabic "NO" before slamming the door in our faces.

As Mam trudged back down the path disconsolately, Athaliah swiftly flung two full milk bottles from the step into the hedge, where they landed with a satisfying thud. Bringing up the rear of the procession down the path, Amerdine used both hands simultaneously to de-head the last few "everlasting" flowers bordering the path, and, with a "May the Lord put a pox on that old heap o' misery", forcefully slammed the gate.

Twisting the pram homeward, Mam decided to call at the Post office to stock up on a quarter of tea and a chocolate for her little helpers. Mrs Mathers, the post mistress knew Mam of old and on entering the low ceilinged interior appeared from behind the post office partition with a smile of recognition. Positioning the final hazel basket invitingly on the counter, Mam placed her order for a packet of Brook Bond. She was served with a neatly wrapped green paper package with a perforated orange savings stamp affixed to the side. An accumulation of these stamps reportedly resulted in a free package, but it was a long time in the coming. Inside the packet, secreted amongst the loose tea leaves were collectors' cards on various themes, numbered to make sets. All selling gimmicks still used to varying degrees even today.

Mrs Mathers surveyed the basket admiringly: "Pretty aren't they, reminds you Christmas is just round the corner."

"It's the last one mind, sold like hot cakes they have today and reasonably priced for the work that's gone into 'em ain't that right girls?"

Athalia and Amerdine nodded vigorously in unison, giving appreciative glances at the by now rather travel weary basket and its lopsided teazle. Following the direction of their gaze Mam's expert fingers did a swift refresher course reverently adjusting the foliage.

"How much are they then?" the post mistress asked.

Quickly totting up in her head the cost of the tea, some sweets and a loaf of bread, Mam offered a reduction "it being the last one" and still left the shop with some silver and her groceries paid for.

"Right my lasses, lets head for home, we've shown 'em how it's done."

Stowing her purchases in the pram, along with the day's cadgings, she balanced her basket on top and with a girl on each arm, stepped out smartly for home, bouncing me along the potholes still holding tight to a turnip and a fruitcake. A chill was descending on the afternoon despite it being but two o'clock. A lone black Austin 7 crunched past and we all stood aside to "watch out for the car." Apart from this, the road was nearly deserted. Buses only ran on Saturdays and most blokes got about a bit on bike or walked. A few fortunates had a ramshackle motor bike, accommodating a wife and off-spring in the attached "sidecar". By and large, motor cars were the province of doctors, nurses, clergy, farmers and landowners and the very well off. Travellers that owned them usually came in at the lower end of the scale and had to make do with cheaper second hand models. It is a testament to their adaptability and skills that with a bit of adjustment and an oily rag, these young men soon got the hang of how to coax the best out of their engines.

By the time we'd trundled home, Dad and Nos Nos had a bright fire waiting and were sat perched on oil drums expectantly, washed and Brylcreamed like lords of the manor.

In our absence, they had had a visit from an old couple we called the down and outs, who trundled round the county with their meagre belongings piled on a perambulator, sleeping under hedges or in barns and begging what they could to get by on. The woman, in her late 50s perhaps, would engage a likely benefactor with, "We're down and we're out of our luck" schpeel, accompanied with much sympathy seeking activity. Her partner would unfailingly complement this with ingratiating tactics and a perfunctory attempt at odd jobbing. Dad always maintained civility but avoided contact with the down and outs, believing the circumstances to which their economy had descended may carry a degree of infection which he did not want his family to catch.

They were also known to try and squeeze themselves in at farms where there was known to be land work available, more hands making lighter work — and lighter pay packets for us.

Mam packed away the remaining unsold pegs against her store of stock for another day's trading remarking "at least they eat nowt". Before long we had a sizzling supper of liver and onions in the pan with chunks of fresh bread to dip in the rich gravy. Afterwards, Pow Pow's cake, cut and sliced, spicy and well packed with fruit evidenced well her baking skills and as Dad commented, "'Er's no work of art, but 'er can't half bake."

8
Ponto's Place

The days that followed fitted into a similar routine, until but a few days before Christmas. Dad had cut a small fir tree which he sharpened the end of and stuck firmly into the ground near the hedge. Knowing this would be my first Christmas, Mam wanted to make it special, so little beads and trinkets were tied about its branches — at last we had a tree! How fragile it looked, twinkling and sparkling in the firelight, this symbol of Our Lord adorning the verge.

Mam made efforts to start and "put things by", out of sight of Dad and his temptations! Pickled onions, pickled cabbage and a packet of dates were secreted away along with a large hand-raised pork pie and some tasty cheese.

While Mam concentrated on her *vittles**, Dad made sure we had churns full of water, a fine pile of fire wood, and oil for the lamp. Dads shopping days were fewer and farther between than Mams, but on the day before Christmas Eve he put on a fresh *diklo** and polished his boots before wrapping me in a blanket and declaring, "We was off out for a bit". Outings with Dad were adventures without structure, journeys into the unexpected. Being carried down the road, held high on Dad's shoulder was a rare treat. Raising his hand to Nellie Pugh, he spied "Pow Pow's blingo" and the lady of the house pinning out her washing. Unable to contain himself from a low whistle followed by an, "Are your buns fresh love?" Turning as fast as size would allow, a delicate flush graced her cheeks and she waved a finger in the direction of his retreating figure, "I'll be tellin' your Mrs about you, you cheeky bugger", to which Dad said, "That's made 'er day".

Next, we called in at Ponto's. Ponto was an old man, maybe in his late 60s. He lived next to Tolley's garage, on a patch of ground in a corner edged by trees. His abode was a four wheeled roadmans hut with a long metal chimney. Dressed in an aged suit that had reached the shiny stage and a collarless shirt, he wore waistcoat, a flat cap and braces. Inside the hut on wheels, a fire blazed in the grate, and it was unbearably warm.

In later years I was grateful to be able to avoid the heat and investigate the flattened cinder-patch round about. A midden was home to a deep ash heap, studded with pilchard tins and jam jars. On the top precariously perched was an enamel chamber pot or "goes under".

Bean poles were propped in the forks of plum trees and various hole bottomed buckets were tactically placed in situations best placed for them to force his rhubarb. A few chickens scratched aimlessly in the sooty soil and pecked at shrivelled damsons. The dark interior of Ponto's home, made discerning detail difficult, but he was good company for Dad, and I was soon lulled to sleep by the murmur of conversation and the heat. When I awoke, Ponto's was receding into the distance and Dad had left a metal paraffin can at Tolley's garage to be paid for and collected later.

It didn't pay a girl to close her eyes round these parts, blink and you'd missed it.

Our next stopping off point was the ancient cottage of Geoff Osborne, set amid a sea of scythed grass, home to apple trees and honey bees, judging by the white hives studded around. Geoff was about the same age as Dad and shared his vast knowledge and deep love and respect for the countryside. Grafton Wood ran to some 139 acres of mature oak woodland, divided into sections by rides. Geoff Osborne (brother of "her of the unrequited love") was head woods man. His cottage was skirted round with evidence of his coppicing and pollarding work. Neat bundles of pea sticks, bean poles, hedge poles and fruit poles, stacked up with brush wood, kindling sticks and fire wood, evidenced his craft. Adept at hedge laying and hurdle making he could also fashion trugs and baskets from steamed wood split into strips. Like Dad, he shared an interest in the habits of the wild animals and could remember the village when, "There weren't even a tractor in sight."

Geoff supplied fresh rabbit at three shillings a pair to local housewives, and had a fine lurcher dog that assisted in this lucrative side line. After an assurance Dad and Nos Nos could continue their arrangement of peg wood collecting, Dad tactically produced two dozen of his best, by way of a thank you, easing out "exchange is no robbery" as he laid them on the table. Mr Osborne ensured

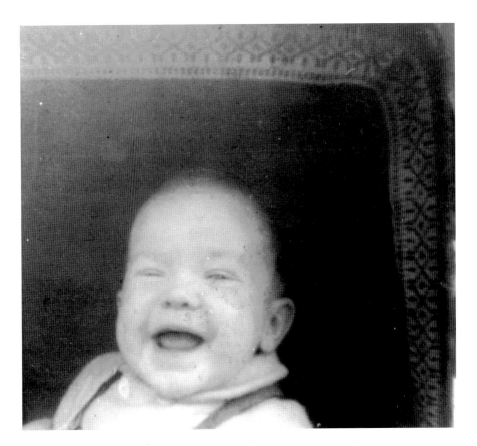

that a bottle of elderberry wine filled the void left by the pegs...
and so it went on, this rhythm of rural recreation, one good turn
deserving another and so on and so on. Just as favours and goodwill were recycled, so was manure and soot, sheep's wool and
feathers, supplying demand and meeting need.

What Dad needed was a last minute present for Mam which
would make her feel like she had been given the earth without
costing it. Mrs Mather's Post Office might be able to supply just
such a need. As the door opened, a bell jingled and the post mistress, more used to serving Mam, raised her eyes in surprise. The
blanket in which I'd been swaddled had unravelled itself during
our wanderings and now mostly entwined itself round Dads leg,
though he didn't seem to have noticed.

With pixie hood askew, covering one eye, and a running nose
that had broken into a gallop, I must have looked a sorry sight.

"What can I help you with?" asked the post mistress, as if not knowing where to start.

Dad explained that he wanted "a bit o' summat for the Mrs and a card to pay me respects", then ruefully inspected the dilapidated state of his baby daughter.

"I'll tell you what, why don't you choose a card while I see to the little 'un for you — they do take some minding don't they?" With this, Mrs Mathers relieved him of his charge and proceeded to spread eagle me on the counter with the practised ease of a professional. With one hand I was subjected to a "spit wash" with a Kleenex — the 1950's answer to a baby-wipe, then reswaddled in the blanket and with hood repositioned and full vision restored, a "rhubarb and custard" lollypop was stuck in my mouth and I was handed back.

By this time, Dad had chosen a pretty card covered in red roses with *Birthday Greetings* emblazoned round the stems. Mrs Mathers raised her other eyebrow but made no comment, tactfully guiding Dads choice of gift away from a "Berrows Journal" and a box of snuff, in favour of a box of Milk Tray, a tub of Atrixo, handcream, a tube of Odour-o-no de-odorant and a bottle of Babycham — "the little drink with the big kick". These purchases she discreetly wrapped before opening the door helpfully to see us on our way, discretion assured.

Striding confidently home, with arms aching, pockets bulging and a distinct whiff of paraffin from the oil can we had collected en route, Dad broadcast his good humour by whistling loudly in step to his walk, old army habits dying hard.

He was still whistling "It's a long way to Tipperary" when we got back to camp.

"It's a bloody long way to Grafton an' all, the time yous have took", greeted Mam, having grown anxious at our extended absence. "Gone all day an not a thought for that babby, she'll be soaking."

"Well you'm wrong there, clever clogs, 'cos taint rained all day" and then to me. *A Dik acoi, mandy's rackli** ...this is all the thanks we get after all the effort we'm made, come back 'ere to pure rottenness."

"Pure rottenness is it?" queried Mam, somewhat taken aback at no indication of contrition at all, reaching out her arms to get hold of me, then patting my padded rear end expectantly. The resulting squelshiness and eye watering odour of ammonia confirmed her maternal suspicions. "Come 'ere my babby 'e aint fit t'ave you, wots ever a state to bring you's back in." It fell on deaf ears. Hiding his "hoard" on the waggon cratch Dad loosed his long dogs and sauntered of to check 'is 'osses, but not without a parting shot across Mams bows to inform her she was "Proper putrefied".

While Dad had been away, Mam had cleaned up and "dabbed a bit o' washing out" then put her dinner on the fire to simmer slowly.

After washing and brushing out her long hair it had been rebraided and putting on a fresh pinnie and a "dab o' scent" she felt assured and refreshed. Mam rarely had time for herself to do as she pleased and secretly enjoyed this lack of responsibility. For Gypsy women with no playpen or garden fence to contain their offspring, it required constant unwavering alertness to ensure safety when stopping near the road.

Added to this, the effort to keep toddlers clean in such basic conditions meant they'd either to be continuously passed round or strapped in their pram, the latter choice rarely sitting easy with the child. The alternative to this was tethering (which may have been a solution on clean grass on a summers day but would beggar belief in the mud of mid winter) or calling on the services of older children to watch the babby. This latter option resulted in girls as young as seven or eight being practiced in the maternal skills of balancing a babe on the hip at the same time as shushing and administering a titty bottle.

Far from being a hardship, the girls usually enjoyed being entrusted with a real babe as opposed to a doll, and "when two or three were gathered together" had a crèche, embellishing the theme of motherhood with the addition of high heels and handbags and a nice string of beads to complete the outfit and all the mannerisms this entailed.

Having dealt with the domestics and the details of her appearance, that natural condiment to Christmas, delicious anticipation took over. Each year having opened our few presents with care, Mam would retrieve the scraps of wrapping paper and run over them with the iron to remove the creases. They were then stored under her mattress till the following year. On this day the "eve of the eve" it was to this stationary horde that she turned, laying her gifts out upon the bed and choosing which item would fit which scrap of paper, then wrapping and re-fixing with precious squares of sellotape, all the while glancing lane-ward to ensure we didn't take her unawares and unwittingly spoil our surprises.

With her wrapping completed, gifts were stored at the bottom of my cupboard bed where prying eyes were least likely to look. She then turned her attention to some goose fat which had been warming on the stove and having ensured that all the contents had melted, took down from the waggon doorway a bunch of hairy comfrey leaves, that had been collected whilst out on a recent hawking trip. Using her bread board and knife to chop the plant finely, this was added to the fat, then stirred gently over a very low heat. While the leaves were infusing she washed and dried an assortment of Shippams paste jars and set them before the stove to warm so as to avoid cracking when the warm liquid was added. Finally, straining the liquid through a clean handkerchief she set the jars to cool and cut circles of coloured paper to be used as decorative lids secured with elastic bands. The resultant comfrey salve could be sold, swapped or gifted away for presents. It was inexpensive to produce and effective to use, known by its country name knitbone and containing significant levels of allantoin, it offered therapeutic benefits for ailments ranging from bronchial problems, sprains and arthritis to skin conditions such as burns, acne and rashes. It reputedly had bone and tooth building properties especially for children. Particularly soothing in winter for chapped hands and rough skin, most could, as Dad put it "find somewhere to dab a bit".

At any rate, it entered into the spirit of Christmas in the days before it had been commercialised, when presents fell mostly into the category of useful and homemade or just homemade. The knitted range was particularly in vogue and women's magazines started in mid September offering patterns for hats, mittens, socks and scarves. A whole plethora of pot holders and tea cosies got in on the act as well in those pre-tea bag times.

Wool was still considered a precious commodity and what started life as a jumper could be meticulously unpicked to reinvent itself as a cardigan only to finally metamorphasise again into several gloves and a bobble hat, all this having started out life as a Swaledale sheep. A close associate of the knitting era was cro-chet, though patterns for this were few and far between and most who embraced the craft contented themselves with going round in circles until they exhausted their supply of wool and battle with boredom, before abandoning it to a jumble sale for some other unfortunate to unravel and rework into something snug and serv-iceable.

As the comfrey salve cooled and set, Mam added more goose grease to the pan and with it dry bread crumbs and chopped bacon rind. Lining a white pudding basin with greaseproof paper and adding a length of string, she held the latter in place pouring in the contents of the pan and draping the string over the side. The resulting 'bird cake', when cooled, would be hung in a nearby hedge to afford us hours of pleasure observing at close range the variety of different birds that would come to feed. A birds eye opportunity to appreciate their individual plumage and behav-iour. It was from waiting and watching Mam's 'bird cake' that I learned to recognise the robin and wren, seasonally depicted on Christmas cards and calendars, along with cheeky blue tits and

great tits as well as the timid approach of the elusive goldfinches with their bright flashes and greenfinches, almost canary yellow in feather.

Without television or wireless to distract, we relied much more on our own creativity and imagination to amuse ourselves. So much was learned and so many skills honed that I am now forever grateful that we never benefited from these media modernities. At the time there was only envy though and the wish that I also might be able look in on *Bonanza* and similar shows.

By the time we returned home, Mam had also found time to do a sizzling pan of crispy crusted bubble and squeak which swung idly over the embers in her hoop handled frying pan. The simplest of fare often tastes best and served with a sprinkling of of pepper and crusty bread it was one of Dad's favourites which he ate with relish — Lea and Perrins to be precise.

In between mouthfuls, Dad would recount how Worcestershire Sauce was invented in 1837 by two dispensing chemists, John Wheeley Lea and William Henry Perrins, at 68 Broad Street in Worcester. Such had been the success of the sauce that in 1897 the pair had opened a factory and had been producing the distinctive condiment there ever since. Eventually, in 1930, the business was sold to "HP".

Recently I met a gentleman who's ambition it had been to make and produce a sauce so fine, it outsold even "HP". Levi Roots recounted how he started out in his Mam's kitchen boiling up chilli sauce with the help of his children to sell at the carnival. He even sang a little song about his sauce, accompanying himself on his guitar. This heart warming entrepreneur realised his ambition and last year in 2008 his "Reggie Reggie Sauce" did indeed outsell even the great "HP".

So, with supper eaten and dishes rinsed, we sat by the fire, I wrapped in a blanket on Mam's knee and Dad and Nos Nos enjoying a last smoke before bedtime.

Dad had erected a small bender tent for his visitor which, backed into the wind, offered reasonable shelter. Eight hazel rods had been sharpened at one end to a spike and driven into the soft earth before securing the ends together. Thus lashed, they provided strength enough to support a sheet. In Granny Ethel's day, water resistant woollen blankets or felt would have been stretched across, secured with long mean blackthorns fried in hog fat. Dad used an old canvas from a waggon and tucking it round snugly like a coat, weighted the hem with stones to keep the wind out. Inside thick straw had been lain and atop of that a portion of worn but serviceable Wilton carpet rescued from the tip had been spread. "Dik 'ere me old *mush**," said Dad "Even when we'm in a tent up a roadside us still 'as a bit o' quality about us".

Mam's little meat safe cabinet, with its cabriole legs, supported a candle stick and a pile of woollen blankets and had been acquired to make up a bed, causing Dad to quote jauntily: "I am a Widney blanket original and best, you'll never get cold feet, with me across your chest".

The little shelter, fragile yet effective held a poignant quality, the similarity between that and our Lord's first home being hard to overlook at that time of year.

Thus, with sparks flying from the fire rising heavenward and preparations nearly complete, our little tree twinkled magically in the wind, expectant of the festivity fast approaching.

Christmas Eve broke bright and clear with a lemon sky and a lull in the wind. Last minute shopping and water fetching took up most of the morning and Dad laid straw around the shafts and waggon in an effort to keep the detested and ever encroaching mud at bay. "Uk me, it's getting more like the nativity everyday", said Dad, surveying his handiwork. "All we need now is the three wise men and a donkey".

"Pow Pow's coming down the lane" called out Mam.

"That just leaves the three wise men then" said Dad chuckling.

Pow Pow could be seen making slow headway down the rutted track. A loose cardigan flapped open and on either arm she was burdened with a basket. Still slippered, she kept to the grass in the middle of the track as far as possible. With no free hand to wave, her toothless smile beamed on regardless. "Well now," she uttered breathlessly and after that gave up the attempt at speech and just gasped like a goldfish.

Mam made tea and when sufficiently recovered, her basket revealed a Christmas cake with "Artex" style icing for snow which supported a rather drunken looking plastic Father Christmas and Rudolph who had had one of his antlers snapped off. The trio was completed by a snow man complete with scarf. There was a jar of

homemade green tomato chutney and a biscuit tin filled with sausage rolls. "Season's greetings" our benefactor chirped, as clearly as anyone without teeth can, happy that her gifts were appreciated. In turn, Mam handed out the comfrey salve and Dad, remorseful over his donkey comment, filled her basket with little faggots of kindling wood and a sprig of mistletoe, "Just in case you meet someone on the way home".

After more joviality, we bade our friend good afternoon and with me on hip, Mam walked her back to the top of the lane, glad of some female company after "sufferin' smoke, snuff and sarcasm" from "them at home".

Mam had decided we would attend the Christmas Eve service. Torn between attending the church at White Ladies Aston, or the one at Grafton, her quandary was simplified when the farmer's wife, whilst delivering a roast chicken, stated her own intention of worshiping at Grafton. She agreed to collect Mam and me and convey us there in her car — joy of joys, a ride in a motor! All of a tizz to get ready, Mam polished her shoes and soaped back her hair, then set about my curls with a comb until I whimpered in pain.

"That's enough of that caper now", said Dad who wasn't enamoured with the idea of church at the best of times, unless he was scything grass round the head stones and getting paid for it. "Gorgiafied carry on anyway... just 'cos the Bible says "suffer little children", 'E never made yous responsible for doing it did 'e?"

Knowing Dad might put his foot down and veto the outing altogether, Mam bit her tongue and made do with attaching a bow to my curls and dampening them down with water. Dressed in another knitted number of that era, a "matinee suit" and a lacy shawl, we were ready to depart by the time two flickering headlights bounced up the lane. Ensconced on Mams knee on the back seat, we chugged away to St John the Baptists. With its 14th century tower it had once formed part of the lands of the monastery at Pershore, a parish in the upper division of the "Pershore Hundred". Approaching from the west, the light shed through the stained glass windows glowed an inviting welcome. The Parson, Garfield Francis, had enlisted the services of the village bell-ringers and the five bells, cast in 1676 by John Martin rang out into the night air with a pleasing chime. Somewhat of a humourist John had had two of the bells inscribed thus: "Be known to all that

doth we see, John Martin of Worcester he made we"....and..."All men that hear my roaring sound, repent before ye ly in ground".

Inside the church, the beamed and whitewashed interior had been decorated with boughs of evergreen, laurel, fir, spruce and yew. Garfield, robed and respectful, welcomed his modest flock of country folk. Candles burned on the altar and when the first carol was announced there was much fumbling and fidgeting as the congregation rose to its feet to raise their voices in praise. Following a further carol and a reading, then another prayer, the fidgety flock was dismissed and having done their duty, dispersed homeward to attach stockings to mantle pieces and welcome bearded visitors down their chimneys.

Delivered back to camp by our chauffer, we discovered Dad had trimmed up the waggon with spirals of silver paper and tiny glass blown "wesley bobs" and baubles. Fragile, light catching and beautiful to behold they transformed the interior from mundane to magical. A packet of paper chains had been hastily "licked and sticked" and now hung in uneven loops from the bows.

The down and outs had called in our absence and stayed long enough to relieve Dad of one shilling and sixpence and a jar of comfrey salve, causing Mam to tell him he was a "soft touch and that a fool and his money was soon parted", to which Dad countered, had she, "Forgot the spirit of Christmas, it being greater to give than to receive", then to Nos Nos, "Waste of time sending it to 'kin church when it comes home with that attitude". Mam said "God helps they that helps themselves", referring to our visitors and Dad replied "Well they 'elped their selves to your hointment so I don't know what you'm belly aching about."

In an effort to restore relations, Nos Nos produced a bottle of Mackesons for Mam and bottles of Guinness for himself and Dad. I was rolled up snug into bed and drifted peacefully to sleep to the rise and fall of voices in companionable conversation and the slurping of milk stout.

9
Beer and
Baby Cham

Christmas morning dawned frosty and clear. We all woke early and had the luxury for once of "over laying', knowing that no work needed doing that day. Dad made everybody tea on the stove and I was ecstatic to find that Santa had filled my stocking with a tangerine, a teddy and some crayons. He had also put a tub of bubbles in, and a little glass dome filled with water and pretend snow which, when shaken, fell on a little village with a church and fir trees and a tiny Santa Claus.

Mam opened her presents and shared round the Milk Tray. There was one particular sweet, the chocolate, shaped like a barrel and tasting of lime which was my particular favourite for many years, until they discontinued it. Childlike herself, Mam sniffed the "Odour-o-no" appreciatively, then tried a dab of Atrixo on the back of her rough hand, before declaring herself "right pleased". Everybody seemed to be smiling and very happy. Dad had a new *diklo**, razor blades and a copy of *Old Moore's Almanac*.

In subsequent decades *Old Moore's* declined in popularity. First published by Francis Moore in the late 1600s these pamphlets contained a ragbag of handy hints ranging from how to plant cabbages and seduce handsome women to curing toothache and subduing an unruly wife. Apparently the constellations, when consulted and carefully calculated, could counsel on omens of flood, storm and earthquake. Dad would peruse these particular periodicals, thinking up ideas and inspirations. If Mam interrupted him during these episodes he would respond with, "Can't you see I am having an idea?" a concept she found hard to challenge.

Nos Nos's presents contained the same gifts as Dad's — bar the *Almanac*. The men had bought each other both bottled beer, conveniently, and Nos Nos had bought Mam a set of handkerchiefs edged with white lace and a very new and unexpected commodity- a bunch of plastic roses. Quite where he had come across them was undisclosed but he assured Mam they would never die off or need watering. Mam agreed that they were hard to distinguish from the real thing, roses in December being a rarity. Dad just looked thoughtful.

While Mam put the carrots and the onions into a pheasant stew, Dad took her aside saying quietly, "Them roses will be the end of your bread and butter my gel, once the gorgias get hold o' them, they won't want our wooden flowers or paper ones no more, then what will you use to buy the babby a new bonnet?".

It didn't take long for Dad's line of thinking to cloud Mam's consciousness as well, and they both regarded the posy with suspicion. "What shall we do?" asked Mam. Unclear whether she meant with the posy in particular or the downturn of the family's future finances in general, Dad wasn't sure. He was sure, however, that nothing was going to spoil their day. "Tell you what, leave dinner on quietly an' we will all tek a turn in the woods to work up an happetite".

Mam protested loudly that she couldn't and then did. Uncle Norris adjusted his trilby hat and donned a donkey jacket. Mam dug out her tweed coat from the cratch and wound a shawl around her shoulders, slipping feet into suede bootees with a zip up the front, a sin to look at but serviceable in slippy weather. Bundled in blankets I started off with Mam, passed up and down the line like a collection plate. "Me arm's fit to burst, this babby is getting heavy." Walking through the grass, stiff and white with ice, past the tethered cobs, the crests of their manes and their moustaches, frosted also. We disturbed a pheasant which winged away heavily, calling warnings of alarm and across a field a vixen stopped in her tracks to listen and watch, before continuing on her way.

Over a criss-cross style encrusted with moss, and at pains to avoid the mud at the gateway, we found ourselves at the start of a woodland ride. These tracks, just wide enough to take a horse and cart or latterly a tractor, were used to access Grafton Woods to let the wood cutters in and felled timber out. They ran across the wood at various angles, tree lined but undergrowth free. Either side showed rutted tyre tracks and in the middle hoof marks where horses had been ridden, probably by the local hunt. Using the ride as an inroad, we walked a short way before taking a deer path to our right, entering the wood proper. The narrow-

ness of the path now allowed only for single file progress, a chance to admire the green textured trunks of the oak trees and the rich peaty soil with it's scent of decaying leaves as they crunched under foot. Occasional clumps of pigeons feathers would suggest a vixen and her quarry had coincided or maybe a kestrel or hunting hawk. Passing a black water pond, weed less and clear, reed fringed, a startled pair of mallards rose rapidly from their reverie, flapping effortlessly out of sight.

"Now if I 'ad me catapult...," said Dad — who had, but didn't want to upset Mam so soon after the roses incident.

Past the pond, we came across a clearing with a little woven hurdle structure with honeysuckle stalks and briar roses twined round it. Inside were three logs stood on end and the evidence of charcoal nuggets from a fire.

"So this is where old Osborne 'ides 'isself," said Dad crumpling paper from his pocket into a ball. Striking a "England's Glory," the paper was soon burning brightly with twigs added, then larger sticks, we soon had a good fire. "We'll just 'av a bit of a warm an I'll 'av a smoke an' we"ll 'ed for 'ome". Mam swept together a heap of dry leaves and laid me on top, glad to give everybody's arms a rest. While they each took rest on a log, I lay on a soft bed of natures providing and watched the blue smoke curl lazily upwards through the cobweb of branches to the December sky. The hush of the wood enveloped us, hugging us to her like a jealous mother her only child. Christmas, pheasant stew, plastic roses, Grafton, Droitwich, Brum — all seemed a world away. Dad was inspecting a grey armour backed woodlouse. "This little bugger's got some sets of legs, look." as he rolled it in the palm of his hand till it curled into a tiny lead like ball.

Respite over, we set off for the walk back home, coming out of the wood near the giant's chair, a huge oak tree stump with upright strut shaped like an armchair. "Watch out for they giants now," Mam warned — and I did, on that occasion and for many years to come — a testament to the power of parental suggestion and a small child's woefully gullible imagination. I didn't just think there may be giants, I knew, and was fearful accordingly, whenever I had to cross that particular field.

Hunger hurried our footsteps homeward. In those days, whenever we returned home, it was with the certainty that everything would be found precisely as we had left it. Gorgias didn't venture round Gypsy stopping places and Travellers didn't thieve from other Travellers, it simply wasn't done. It can be argued that those were thriftier more austere times and few families had the trappings then that many have today but even so there existed a loyalty of sorts which has now sadly declined.

The Romany race has been diluted with gorgia blood. Still more concerning are the middleclass artists and trendies who purport to other middleclass artists and trendies to themselves be Travellers and attempt, rather unconvincingly in most cases, to society at large, to pass themselves off as such, even in the face of overwhelming evidence to the contrary.

Once home, Mam ladled out aromatic pheasant stew. While that was consumed she carved slices of meat from the donated chicken. Diced potatoes were fast fried in hot dripping fat and a brisk boiling of sprouts were served with gravy. Mam had a habit of adding a pinch of bicarbonate of soda to the brassica's she boiled. It turned them an unnaturally garish shade of green and successfully reduced their vitamin value to virtually nil.

With main course disposed of and Mam declaring we were that greedy, "We could eat one more 'tater' than a pig," she turned her culinary attentions to the Christmas pudding. Fruit rich and spicy it bubbled in a pudding cloth at the side of the fire, to be served companioned by custard — Birds Eye — less likely to lump.

Our meal that day was reminiscent of an "Ethel effort," which Mam in turn had passed on. Not all Travellers would have had our varied diet and for many it would have been bacon as usual. even on this day of national celebration.

In the afternoon, while we let our dinner settle, I played with my new toys and beautiful bubbles were blown which wafted gently upward and across the lane to expire defencelessly with a pop on the prickles of the hawthorn hedge.

Mam shared round more Milk Tray and wished she hadn't.

The box was emptying rapidly, even the hard ones falling victim to Dads sweet tooth. "Them Cadburys like us sort a people," said Dad "I knows that for a fact, an' them Rowntree's too" With this he bit hard into on another caramel, positioning it expertly between two molars to get a better grip. "Must be on account of how you boost their profits," answered Mam. "He'll 'av' read it in 'is halmanac," piped up Norris. "That's how 'e knows."

During the afternoon, visitors came and went, perhaps enjoying a drink with us or a piece of cake, all enjoying the fire and the company and a day when no-one expected to be moved on or shifted. By evening, all had departed to their own respective firesides — those newly esconsed in trailers had gone to ignite the calor gas, a soulless but instant output of heat.

With horses hayed and watered for the night, Mam took a bone handled knife from the champagne pot and cut portions of pork pie to partner pickles and cheese served on her best china plates. Beer and Babychamp completed the celebration and my first Christmas, the last of the decade, drew peaceably to a close.

10
White Drops and
Yellow Dills

Directly after New Year, we awoke one frost filled morning to find Uncle Norris had departed in the night. His blankets were left neatly folded on the straw in the "bender" and two bottles of Mackeson's and ten Woodbine balanced reverentially on top.

No-one had been aware of his secret silent departure but all appreciated how the sadness of an impending farewell had been adeptly avoided – at least for the dearly departed. Mam and Dad were left feeling bereft and listless, habit causing them to glance intermittently up the lane, though knowing in their hearts that he had gone.

There's something about being the ones left behind that initiates discontent and restlessness , frequently only dispellable by those remaining themselves packing up and leaving the area also. Early January is neither the best time to be shifting nor the easiest time to be earning a living. Those *gorgias* who had recently over-extended their expenditure at Christmas were now less eager or willing to be parted from their pounds. Travellers taking to the road risked an even more uncertain reception than usual.

Balanced against this was the need to dispel the imposed bout of melancholy and action was the antidote.

The rag and bone round, immortalised by Wilfred Bramble and Harry H. Corbett in *Steptoe and Son* was an urban exercise best practised on the cobbled streets of back-to-back industrial and semi-urban areas. Too far away in their rural setting from suitable rag merchants with whom to "weigh in," Mam had nevertheless found a company who conducted their business via the Royal Mail. "Send-us-wools" would receive parcels of woollens through the post from reliable sources. The company, on receipt of the parcel would check and weigh the contents and then despatch a postal order by return for the price of the woollens, including a refund for the original postage costs. It sounds a laborious process now, but fifty years ago it provided a lucrative side-line for Mam. The reason many Travellers didn't embark on the exercise was either their lack of literacy, woollens or a postal address. Mam was the proud possessor of all three which gave her a head start in the venture.

Collecting or cadging her woollens whilst out hawking or clearing the remains of jumble sales for free, ripping open the linings of coats to fill them with garments which Dad would collect later, piled high on the pony and cart, she had a ready supply. Adept at assessing which fabrics were pure wool and which were not, Mam would sort them into piles on the grass verge ready for despatch. Paper spud bags and bailer twine were readily available from local farms and with the aid of sealing wax, sellotape and a bic biro she was in business. Once the parcels were despatched, Mam had only to wait for the return of the payments. These, over our stay at Grafton, had been sent c/o Mrs. Mathers at the Post Office. Following Mam's instructions she had stored them there uncashed until such a time as we were ready to "pull off" and take with us Mam's nest egg or as Dad called it, "a nice little earner".

Dismantling the recently vacated bender and consigning all but essentials to the "pyre fire", we again prepared to shift. The tree, when burned, sparked and crackled with pine sap and the "wesley bobs" were rewrapped in thin tissue and packed in an Oxo tin ready for next year. Horses were brushed over and harness oiled, this being an anticipated rather than an enforced departure there was more time to prepare.

On the 'eve of the leave' Mam settled me in the pram and we set off for the mile walk to the post office to collect our wool money and to see if any of Mam's "snaps" had been delivered.

One of the things about memories is that you can't always remember when you first started remembering, nor exactly the order in which early events took place. Also I think there may be some overlapping between how we were told things happened and what exactly we recall. I do remember being in my first pram and recently, when out scrapping, one of my children collected a pram, exactly the same model and make as I had been a passenger in some half century before. As a baby, much of my time was spent in a pram in a field, be it peas, strawberries, cabbage or mangolds. As well as recollections of this I also have photographs. Probably my earliest clear memories were when I was about two or three. These remembrances have been kept clear and lucid with the aid of a small collection of family photographs which my Mam guarded as being very precious, as indeed they were. The clear sharp images are in the minority and they are the ones that professional photographers have taken. The blurred fuzzy ones are my Mam's attempts with the camera, capturing more mundane moments in our life, usually at a strange angle.

I can still remember the drawn out process of acquiring these photographs or snaps as they were called in the 1960s. First she would take the pictures, using a square box camera, then a visit to the Post Mistress at Grafton Flyford. Here, the obliging post mistress would attempt to extricate the film spool from the camera in the darkness of the coal shed, to avoid over-exposure, a term which was lost on us but sounded well worth avoiding. This hopefully unexposed film would then be despatched by mail to a firm called Gratispool. When this firm had printed the pictures, all in black and white and bordered with white edges, they were reposted back to the post office ready for collection. We might have travelled some distance away in the intervening time, in which case they would be stored next to the bacon slicer ready for collection. Mrs Mathers would send a message — with Percy the road sweeper – whose calling meant he got about a bit and when our routes eventually coincided, he'd relay the message "dem yur, dem dur" which roughly translated meant the snaps were ready. He was a man of few words was Percy and most of them were unintelligible. The bacon-scented snaps were eagerly collected and temptingly un-viewed until the journey home completed and all assembled for the unveiling. Even Dad, not one for "fanglements and trinklements", his phrase for most things modern, mechanical and mysterious would stop whatever he wasn't really doing to be there, hopefully, for the display. Out of a possible twelve pictures (we had a thing called a dozen in pre-decimal days) half would be blurred or blank and the rest showed deadpan faces, devoid of expression or evidencing signs of fidgeting where the subjects had been unable to hold the pose long enough for the shutter to click. "'Kin waste of time" dad would gloat with satisfaction, secretly pleased with the cameras lack of success and the pronounced futility of the whole exercise. "'Kin good job they sent a spare film then," Mam would retort, determined to continue until the technique was mastered. "...Best thing a-going is a camera..."

With all other little transactions and arrangements complete it would be "early to bed and early to rise, takes them gorgias by surprise".

Shifting usually evoked a conflict of emotions, regret at what was being left behind infused with anticipation for the unknown that lay ahead.

In this case it was Barrow-on Trent.

Our journey was to take us on a round-about route through the shires of Gloucester and Derby, some two hundred miles of which Mam would walk, most of it as a pedestrian with a pram, the tyres on the wheels being markedly thinner when we reached our destination, as probably was my Mam.

Dad usually delayed his first "shift" of the year until early February, as by Valentines Day he usually reckoned to have "fell in love with the new year," having reached the point where he hoped the worst of the winter was behind us.

The departing Norris had forced his hand and having taken the plunge to pull away, he had to keep swimming, regardless of the ebb and flow of fortune's tide. With enough put by to see us

through a few weeks, most of the time was spent travelling and trying to keep warm, hence more time spent in the confines of the waggon. It was then I learned to walk, from one toddling step to another, holding onto lockers and bunks for support. At the age of nine months, I was finally on the move and by and large have stayed that way ever since. Spring came early that year and I had a birds-eye view as it gloriously unfolded. It is still, without exception my favourite time of year, full as it is of promise and reward after so much waiting and anticipation. I defy anyone not to feel delight at the first sign of snowdrops rising valiantly from frozen earth through a carpet of moss, to hang their green and white frilled heads like debutantes, pure yet hopeful.

While my infant eyes beheld beauty, Mam and Dad's beheld bounty — and profit. "See nature and pick it."

From our new stopping place "white-drop" picking began.

We were pulled with a handful of families, still at that time themselves in waggons, each united by the same purpose. Early each morning, armed with "chip" baskets, lightly constructed of slivers of wood or hard card, with tin handles, the onslaught on the white-drops began. Long stalks with budded heads were deftly bunched and banded to be packed upright in moist moss and hawked around the towns. For those far removed from rural signs of spring, they found a ready market at 6d a bunch or 3 bunches for a shilling, which was twelve old pence. Pickers with nimble fingers or able children would work crouched low amid a sea of snowdrops and cellandines, "silver and gold', jewels in the winters dry leaves. Dogs mercury and lords and ladies with their furled spikes unfolding to shiny glossed spade shaped leaves added splashes of green to nature's palette.

For those too far from towns to make door to door selling a viable option, the bunches were packed in wooden tomato boxes and sent on the morning milk train to the cities or Covent Garden to be collected by eager flower sellers or wholesalers. Today, it would doubtless be considered desecration, but back then it was classed as survival and nature's offerings deemed freely available for the taking, much as blackberries still are today.

In Gloucester, the county we were heading for next, the Dymock yellowdills, a small hardy native variety of daffodil, suffered a similar fate. Anyone wanting to find the whereabouts of the nearest Gypsy camp had only to follow the trail of discarded and wilting flowers to be directed to their desired destination.

The woodland anemone that shared this blooming time was spared its delicate shell pink flowers by dint of the fact it wilted so easily. As in life, an early 'wilter' wouldn't stay the course.

After a dawn rise for picking and an early start for a day's hawking with baskets of flowers, the women were all back at camp by early afternoon to check their fires were 'agoing' and cooking pots were on the simmer.

Old Fliddy – alas dead these many years – no longer went out with her basket, preferring to stay round her waggon and watch the camp or mind younger children whose mothers had gone out calling. Content to pass her day keeping an eye on the tethered horses or stick gathering for her fire she had for company two miniature "tea-cup" dogs of diminutive size which tripped at her button booted heels wherever she went.

Her waggon was immaculately kept and on a sunny day she laundered her linens and lace before bleaching them in the sun to dry. Her little chamfered china cabinet was packed with fine bone china cups and saucers. Shelves displayed old family snaps of relatives long departed.

On afternoons, knowing she "favoured a bit o' civil company wi' sensible people" Mam would be invited to 'come up' into Fliddy's waggon to, "Take a basin of tea with an old widow woman what's more time as she knows what to do with." As a babe I was included in these select afternoon soirées but later years resulted in being banished to "go out now to they big bits o' gels".

Old Fliddy prepared parchment thin salmon sandwiches and buttered Gypsy cakes* baked on her griddle and wrapped still warm in a 'muslin'. While Mam sipped Earl Grey from the hallowed crockery she admired the assembly of family likenesses, a favourite subject which Fliddy never tired of exploring though her visitors found slightly depressing.

"Who's that then Aunt?" Mam would indicate a sepia figure in a silver filigree frame. "Well now me dear, that's my Nelson as took old Samson's gel Leander — he's dead now..." "Ah, I'm sorry to hear that," Mam would console, then moving swiftly on "what about this one here, who's this?" "That's me sister Lavinia , passed away in '56, God love her." Almost all of the pictures transpired to

97

be of people now "passed over". This spirited and courageous lady had out lived so many who had upped and gone before.

It was to be wondered if she had quite forgiven them for forsaking her in favour of their maker, she to remain with only memories of the companions of her day. Fortitude and the love for her children and grandchildren was her motivation. Known for speaking her mind — "what's on me tongue has got to come off" — Fliddy was nevertheless much cared for and respected. Admired for being a proper old fashioned Traveller, an hour spent in her company constituted a genteel and pleasurable interlude. Mam and I departed our afternoon tea party, refreshed by her kindness as well as her tea.

Shortly after our spell on the whitedrops, Dad continued our journey to Barrow-on-Trent. We found ourselves pulled on a piece of ground adjacent to the canal near Bethel. "We shall arise and go up to Bethel," quoted Mam, who had some fair rememberings of Bible passages considering I never saw her reading one. The spiritual significance of the place became more evident a few days later when the local Methodist Minister happened by and spotted Mam "dabbing out" her washing, with me hobbling her knees. Dad quite liked the old man with his pressed crease trousers and shining leather shoes. "You can tell a lot by how a man keeps 'is boots", Dad reckoned. He'd taken a shine to the clergyman who had taken a shine to his shoes. Dad enquired if Mr Kinchington would come down the lane to "christen the babby" and it was arranged that the roadside ceremony would take place the following Saturday.

"Do yous reckon he'll turn up?" remarked Mam, calculating how *ladging** it would be in front of friends and family if the cleric did not materialise.

"Don't reckon he'm the flakey type," was Dad's diagnosis. In those days flakey was a term denoting someone shallow, many faceted, two faced, or likely to "cock of" on a deal. "Don't pay no 'eed to 'e, 'em as flakey as the pastry on a pasty", meant an individual unworthy of trust, any dealings with whom were likely to end in disappointment.

Mr Kinchington, as good as his word and equally fond of babies, duly attended and carried out his duties. With a motley assortment for a congregation and a cut glass bowl for a font he exercised the power vested in him by Bethel Methodist Church,

christening me and adding another little itinerant soul of no-fixed-abode to the cradle roll of those blessed, dedicated and saved.

With the ceremony concluded and the vicar vacating, a bee-line was made for the Cat and Fiddle Public House for some singing and supping to celebrate. As the star of the show, I was wrapped up in a blanket and put in the landlady's parlour, thereby missing the festivities entirely.

Mam and Dad had walked near on two hundred miles to mark this rite of passage and after a well earned trip to the Crown Derby Works on Osmaston Road, where Dad "tret" Mam to a little "reminder of the hoccassion", we went back to our pull-in at Barrow, Mam hugging close her prized present.

Crown Derby china is highly sought after by Travellers and the 'Old Imari' or cigarette pattern a particular favourite. Mam didn't have much, but the few bits of things she did have were precious. In Mam's eyes 'it showed a bit o' class'.

11
Give Us This Day
Our Daily Bread

The weather held fine and while Dad made plans to make his way back to "the Vale", Mam took time to catch up on her wifely duties. Having worked her way through a pile of washing, she retrieved it item by item, still determined but damp from the bramble hedge and set about pressing it. With the aid of two flat irons and a trivet, she heated one iron at the fire while wielding the other in her hand. A bushel box with a blanket formed her ironing board and kneeling in the grass she skimmed over my dainty cotton dresses, her blouses and Dads *diklos**. Two pairs of socks covered her right hand to insulate the heat from the hot iron handle and by dint of 'spit and sizzle' she would access whether or not the smoothing iron was hot enough to remove the creases without being so hot as to burn the fabric. Lack of judgement or loss of concentration resulted in a brown triangular scorch mark accompanied by an unmistakable smell of singed cloth.

While Mam ironed, Dad set about burnishing our steel "jacks", bowls and iron pots. Using moistened wood ash or brick dust he would dampen a rag then rub away at stubborn stains on the metal, to finish off burnishing brightly with one of Mam's old vests.

"'Mazin' what a difference a bit of spit and polish makes". By now fully mobile, I got enjoyment from these humbler signs of domestic activity, a joy and appreciation in taking care of things and a pride in their appearance.

"Folks can tell a lot about yous by the way yous tek care of your stuff", Dad counselled. He was right, and his words so true. What a person is on the outside becomes evident on the outside. A wise lesson for a child and a useful one for a fortune teller, often considered with awe for being able to read 'em like a book.

With my little frocks all pressed, Mam had taken the notion to trim up my outfits with ribbons and bows. As well as these millinery measures, she also went to pains to sew tiny silver bells to my pockets. Thus when she was working she would know without looking up that I was still nearby, from the tinkling sound they gave off. No tinkling meant I had wandered out of range or was motionless asleep. She was interrupted in her stitching by the arrival by horse and dray of a be-hatted Travelling man, past middle age, dressed in a check shirt, corduroy trousers and braces. Looking up at the dogs disturbance, Dad muttered " We've got a visitor Missis, it's old "Off-an'-on".

The reason he was so named was based on his frequent assertions that he was permanently tottering on the brink of hard times or even destitution.

"How's it going brother?" asked Dad, looking up from his scouring and indicating a vacant milk crate with a nod of his head. "Off an' on," came the well predicted reply. "Quiet though ain' it? Not a lot about is there?" Mam and Dad thought to the contrary, but agreed nevertheless. Lurching from the dray, which creaked alarmingly, indicating its advanced stage of decay, he looped the reins round the shafts before slipping the looped end over the trace hook, this relaxed approach doubtless designed to show off his faith in his cob's ability to stand. Pulling up the proffered crate, he seated himself with an "I don't know I'm sure." Accepting sweetened tea, there followed a disjointed discourse on the down turn of all events in general and his own in particular. During this time, the cob, by now bored, had stretched its neck far enough to successfully reach some grass to nibble at, snapping the aged leather of the reins in the process. "Is 'e alright that 'oss?" queried Dad. "Aye 'e will be," answered Off-and-on without bothering to look round. Mam and Dad exchanged glances which silently expressed their doubts.

Off-an-on contrived to make dire forecasts on all business ventures imaginable, by which time the cob had moved with halting steps nearer to the narrow canal bridge over which the little lane went.

Oblivious to the widening distance between himself and his turn-out he was stopped mid flow by a cyclist, attired in a bike cape which flapped Batman style behind him, flying past on a bicycle ringing his bell. Startled from its blissful grazing, the frightened animal tried to take flight over the bridge. The unfortunate angle at which it tackled the bridge, however, resulted in a splintering crash followed by a pounding of hooves and a flying tail as the harness parted company from the dray, which was now firmly wedged between the stone sides of the bridge. The terrified horse was seen making his way across a neighbouring field. Off-an'-on craned his neck in the direction of his equipage, managing to stutter, "'Uk me", whilst rising to his feet and adjusting his hat. By now both cob and cyclist were fast disappearing from view. Dad shot a warning look at Mam to contain her amusement, himself turning away to hide an untimely chuckle. The two men between them, managed to drag the dray clear and whilst its unfortunate owner pondered on the impact damage, all the while uttering further oaths, Dad set off across the field with a rope halter and a hunk of bread. A generous gesture of assistance on his part in the face of calamity, it was also a good opportunity to release his mirth in private.

Once danger had diminished, the amiable cob again resumed its placid grazing and was easily recaptured and returned to its disenchanted owner who cursed it soundly. With a hammer and nails, Dad managed to do enough running repairs to get Off-an-on back to his own camp and with wire and bailer band, the tattered harness was cobbled together to provide more service. Reluctantly re-yoked, man and horse departed, the owner declaring "Here's ever a carry on"... and that he would, "Stripe him up proper all the way home"... and how he, "Couldn't abide a 'kin disbehavin' hanimal."

That night, Dad shut the bantams up in their travelling basket when they went to roost, a sure sign that we'd be shifting in the morning, which we did.

Working and wandering our way back through the 'Shires to the Vale', we enjoyed a spring in all it's magical beauty. As the green grass grew, lusher primroses peeped through, fighting for a foothold on life like the new-born lambs that gambolled and graced the pastures we passed, penned in by hedges dangling khaki catkins from brown branched bushes. Mam packed primroses and violet clumps in Dads criss-cross baskets and they graced many a window sill in the villages we passed through, the shillings she charged keeping our food hamper well stocked. The horses' coats lost their winter thickness and from healthful

hedgerow pickings, their coats shone, improved in condition by the regular work in harness. Later in the year, Dad would scythe nettles and then stack them to dry, maintaining that the iron rich fodder encouraged the "five shilling piece marks" on their hind quarters, so indicative of being in the very best of health.

When Dad wasn't packing his pipe with twist and puffing steadily, his whistling inspired cheerful nods and waves. Happiness is indeed infectious, and as evenings drew out, there was an interest and purpose everywhere as the countryside, our home, came back to life.

Distrustful householders still refused us water from time to time, objectionable constables attempted to prove their puny authority but neither had much impact as we were only passing through.

In later years, Brian Vesey Fitzgerald, somewhat of an authority on Gypsy people, remarked that Mam and Dad saw the world through glasses with a rosier tint than most. This was a shrewd observation. Brian had observed that they were of the belief that whilst it is not always possible to choose one's circumstances, it was always possible to choose one's attitude and theirs was mostly a cheerful and humorous one in the face of any adversity, a trait which served them well through the vagaries of travelling life.

Mam collected wild ramsons to flavour her spring broths and stews, warily snipping nettle tops to boil for "Gypsy Spinach', telling me how they "cleant your blood an kep' yous pure".

Dad discarded a layer of winter shirts, consigning them to the fire. Mam burned the worn down bootees and shed her tweed coat.

In the evenings, from a vantage point on Dad's shoulder, we'd peer in the hedges for birds nests which he would place in my chubby hand, to observe their colour and size before gently returning them to moss-filled nests for the hen birds to re-sit. Winter wheat, now finger high, was a boxing ground for the antics of mad March hares, even in April. Stoats and weasels darted across the road in a flash and Mam would ask Dad, "What's the difference between a stoat and a weasel?" "Well duck, a weasel is weasily identifiable and a stoat is stoatly different". He always called everybody "duck" for ages after we had stopped round Derbyshire.

One day, bored of being strapped in the pram for a day's travelling and driving Mam to her limits of patience with my whinging, she popped my tame chicken Jan Jan in alongside for company. Entertained by my feathered friend I was soon asleep with my head cushioned on her wing. Dad got a shock when he peeled back the blankets to find a chicken and a child, and I got a shock to find she had laid an egg. I had "shock on toast" for tea with soldiers and it was the first of many brown speckled gifts which she gave, becoming a constant companion to confide in with baby chatter. Prepared to be dressed in beads and bonnets, that docile chicken put up with a lot.

On Sunday afternoons, it was the habit for those newly blessed with a motor to go for a ride and to visit those non mechanically equipped, usually with the unspoken intention of showing off. Hence much ado would ensue about where to park it, checking the engine for water or testing the horn.

Two such Sunday visitors were Aunt Rose and Uncle Bill. Though not in the "look at what we've just got" category it did indeed still cause quite a stir when their spacious Morris Oxford — two tone — sleekly pulled up alongside. Two boys, both older than me would slide off the back seat and dive into the bushes, keen to relieve themselves after their journey. Out of the cavernous boot would emerge striped folding chairs and usually a basket of food — guests that came prepared were extra welcome. In any case, in times when no-one had a telephone and shops didn't open on a Sunday, surprise visitors had to make do with just drinking tea if they didn't come equipped to dine.

Uncle Bill had done well for himself but was too well bred to show it, still enjoying a seat, albeit striped, at the roadside fire partaking of frequent mashings of tea. He, Dad and the boys would then set off "wooding" and leave Mam and Aunt Rose to "get girly". Rose had a handbag and what unfathomable mysteries that held. Our en-suite being a bush, I'd escort her to the nearest, then keep watch till the deed was done.

After hand washing, she'd delve into the handbag and produce a round compact filled with powder and a puff, housing a mirror in the lid. If I was in range, which I worked hard at, I'd get a dab of powder on the nose too. She and Mam would rifle through a selection of scent bottles and we would all have a few experimental squirts on the wrist, to be appreciatively sniffed and "oo ahd" about. Next would come tubes of lipstick and aided by the compact mirror I'd pucker up for a shot at that too. Aunt Rose introduced Mam to mascara and they soon made friends. It came in a blue oblong box with a brush and was pressed into a compartment at one side, a bit like boot polish, with a gap where the brush slotted in. Mam was shown how to moisten the cake with a drop of water from the kettle then brush the cosmetic on her eyes for the "spider" effect. It made Mam look a bit wild and startled but we all got used to it and it made her feel made-up.

Later, she did away with the kettle water and just spat on it, as she reckoned it made it spread better. Aunt Rose also wore stockings and painted her toenails, it left those of us that didn't feeling frumpy and plain.

When Dad and his wood carriers got back, they'd regale us with accounts of the badgers sett they'd visited or the jay bird they had seen. "A right little Bramwell Evans", Mam muttered, fluttering her new lashes at Dad and passing him his dish of fresh tea. He accepted but looked disconcerted. In his absence something had changed but he hadn't quite fathomed what it was.

With a cloth spread on a blanket, we sat down for sandwiches and hardboiled eggs. Uncle Bill produced something called an egg slicer. Made of turquoise plastic, it had a shaped dip where the egg was placed for a frame of wires to be closed over it, slicing as it went. We obligingly "ood and ahd" about that as well. Dad looked bemused, thinking his knife would have done it in half the time and asked Bill if he'd a "contraption to shell 'em an all".

Passing round slices of egg the reply was "No". At 'dimsie dark' time, the little family would reload into the Morris Oxford and with parting gifts of comfrey salve or a criss-cross basket on our part and chocolate and edible goodies on theirs, they would cruise away into the dark. The Marshalls were a nice family who had not been spoiled by success. After they had gone, Mam sliced bread and butter and sprinkled the chopped up chocolate on top, it made it go further so we could all have some. The sweet chocolate embedded in the soft salted butter made an interesting contrast.

She had some strange but good ideas, my Mam.

Another experience we had had of plastic, first the artificial roses and now the egg machine, it seemed to be cropping up everywhere in different colours and forms.

As we neared Easter, we also neared the Vale and Dad was faced with a variety of work such as apple tree pruning or hop training to "put us on a bit" till it was time to pull to Eckington or Bideford-on- Avon for the pea-picking.

12
Calor Gas
Cousins

The March winds that had buffeted our waggon so disrespectfully subsided and walks in the bluebell woods were a magical journey. Like the Wood Anemones, they were wilters and luckily so for them, as it meant they escaped the fate of being bunched and hawked. May blossom luxuriated on hawthorn bushes and our canvas roof was showered with winged ash keys. The sky grew bluer and the clouds lighter and whiter as spring progressed.

Uncle Nos Nos re-appeared as silently and unexpectedly as when he had left and Dad erected a bender tent as before, glad to have the return of his partner in crime. To celebrate the reunion of the duo, they strolled down to the Rose and Crown for a pint. Observing a woman busy cleaning her letter box with brasso Dad sang out "Do you want your knockers polished love?" and Nos Nos joined in with "You could give me knob a shine".

Like Butch and Sundance, 'the boys were back in town'.

In the end, Dad opted for a shift to Eckington and we pulled in the gateway of the pea field, with plenty of time before the picking started. Again the crushed camomile released its pungent scent and this time, Mam made sweet tea and flavoured it with honey. She and I enjoyed it but Dad and Norris stuck to Brook Bond with a dash of Tate and Lyle.

Apple blossom time in the Vale was a beauty to behold as orchard upon orchard burst forth in a riot of frothy pink. Bus trips were organised from Brum, so that city unfortunates could enjoy the display, as showy as an Ascot hat. Interspersed with this, were the white and less 'blousy' blossom of the pear trees, both attracting much buzzing of bees with their wealth of pollen. A gentle breeze moving through the branches caused confetti cascades of petals to carpet the grass or blow in drifts across the road. Dandelions opened their faces during daylight hours to brazenly stare at the sun. Dainty daisies dared above the grass, to be adorned as daisy chains by groups of nimble fingered giggling girls.

Gone the tormenting mud, replaced by sandy soil, sensuous to the toes. Butterflies fluttered by unrushed but intent.

There frequented these parts an ancient lady called Miss Ostrahan who had a fascination of sorts for Gypsy people. An invalid of respectable age, she was conveyed around the village in a three wheeled wicker bath chair which she steered with a handle. Propulsion came in the form of a youth called Edwin, who she employed for gardening and other sundry duties.

Miss Ostrahan invoked the same terror that Donkey Lane did, intangible yet potent. On nearing our camp and seeing me playing she would urge Edwin forward into a trot, the better to steer a course in my direction. Too small to run away I was soon cornered by a nettle patch, a victim at her mercy, out numbered and out run. Her black button eyes pierced forcibly and a voice too large for her feeble fray would boom out "We've caught one, Edwin", ... then..., "Speak to me child". At this point she would produce a large and cavernous black ear trumpet swivelled in my direction. Fear of somehow being sucked up the trumpet finally galvanised me into action and I would scramble through the hedge or take my chances with the nettles, only stopping my escape when the sound of Edwin's puffing and the rumble of her wheels were far behind.

Once convinced of her departure, I'd return home to find Mam with beads or humbugs or even once a sequined reticule. "That Miss Ostrahan left these for you", Mam greeted, perplexed at my bramble scratches and tear-stained face. The invalid with evil intent, had even managed to pull the wool over Mam's gullible short sighted eyes.

As apple blossom drifted away so did the delicate pea flowers, replaced by lush pods, popping with peas and curling tendrils. Picking started early in the day and families worked in groups seated on boxes, the uprooted haulms drawn across their knees, secured by the left hand and de-podded by the right. Crates were rapidly filled and stacked in the shade and covered with damp sacks to prevent weight loss through dehydration. Families sipped cold tea and Corona lemonade to prevent a similar fate themselves. Babies strapped in prams invigilated proceedings and toddlers seated in the dust vied for attention. Conversation was interspersed with periods of industrious silence. As the sun rose and the heat of the day intensified, so did the dabbing of foreheads and glances at the church clock. For those who had been on the field since four o'clock, the striking of the noon chime heralded the end of a lucrative and not unenjoyable eight hour day. When the farmer had reckoned up the tally for the day's pickings, workers could opt to be paid on a daily basis or leave wages to accrue till the end of the week.

Dad and uncle usually waited to collect their money daily, while Mam went on ahead to start the tea. Considering Mam's meagre supply of equipment – a few iron pots and an odd assortment of knives, spoons and a tin opener, she accomplished plenty with little. Recently she had added to her armoury a wooden bread board, carved in a circular pattern with ears of wheat and a scriptural suggestion that the dear Lord "Give us this day our daily bread", a nest of three white basins and a wooden rolling pin. Prior to the rolling pin, she had improvised with the use of an old milk bottle.

On our way home from the pea field, she steered the pram in the direction of Mr Bates the "High Quality" butcher. Applying the brake and with my conveyance in a position clearly visible from the inside the shop, Mam disappeared within. Watching her progress across the black and white tiled floor, which was liberally sprinkled with sawdust to catch the blood, I watched as she selected her purchases. Mr Bates, in his blue and white apron and straw boater weighed and wrapped each item. When it came to payment time he deposited coins in an ornate, majestic silver cash register which reigned supreme on the counter, displaying black symbols of 1/- and 1/6d on white cards.

"We'm having a treat tonight my gel", Mam promised as the pram surged forward from her hefty shove. Later she remembered to release the brake and from thereonin the ride got smoother. On arriving home, Mam's rare treat was unwrapped from its grease proof paper, bloodied but proud, rolled and trussed with string then wrapped in a pudding cloth and plunged into boiling water. Later it emerged to be unfettered and pressed into a basin, and with Mam's ingenuity weighed down with her flat iron and plunged into a basin of cold water. While baby beetroot boiled and bobbed in burgundy bliss, Mam gathered fresh watercress, emerald green. Keen to sample this delicacy of Mam's, which warranted subduing with a flat iron I was first for a test taste as her carving knife sliced with ease through the tender pink meat,

111

depositing a sliver in my expectant upturned mouth. The meat melted effortlessly, girded with flavoursome jelly in which it had set, delicious and delicate with a dainty yet distinctive flavour.

"Who else wants some of me tongue?" asked Mam, depositing a slice amid the beetroot and watercress.

"I've been having it all me married life" said Dad holding his hand out for his plate. "Wished it was always offered before it was given and always this enjoyable. I could even get a taste for it."

Dad played to the gallery when Uncle Norris was about.

"Ah but you still love me", said Mam, happy to see Dad enjoying the fruits of her labours.

"Aye", responded Dad, "Like the Devil loves Holy water."

Another of Mam's "basin" recipes which she surprised us with, was summer pudding. Skilled at feeding her family on next to nothing, she cut crusts off sliced white Mothers Pride, then lined a basin with a lightly boiled medley of strawberries, currants and raspberries, sweetening the natural flavour of the juice with a little shake of sugar. Filling the basin with this fanfare of fruit she sealed the top with a lid of bread, to be kept cool and served much later with evaporated milk. These flurries of creative cuisine when Mam had been inspired by some housewives hint or a magazine extravaganza could be interspersed with spells of "taters" cabbage and bacon, monotonous but filling. Occasionally, new fads would hit the market or more truly old ones – of the Mrs Beeton era, revamped by the likes of Fanny Craddock. One such was "marbled jelly". Cheap to make and quick to prepare it consisted of a coloured Chivers jelly mixed at those vital pre setting moments, with the erstwhile ingredient evaporated milk. It graced our table on many a Sunday when visitors were expected.

Misguidedly, liking to imagine herself at the forefront of progress on the pantry front, Mam was soon extolling the virtues of a new forerunner in the field, — Fray Bentos pies. As well as being the name of a South American town in Uruguay, it referred to a company which had been pioneers in the pre-cooked meat industry since 1899. Synonymous with convenience, they had now invented a pie which though a tinned travesty of the real thing never the less offered a new experience to aficionados of steak and kidney pie. Having perfected the art of cooking and tinning meat, they now went on to crown it with pastry and encase it with steel.

Mam extolled the virtues of this new fangled invention and bemoaned the fact that unlike her 'caravan calor gas cousins' she had no oven with which to demonstrate the prowess of the pie. Dad relented and promised to see what he could do. What he managed was a trip to the tip where he "tip scoggled" until finding a metal Fox's biscuit box about a foot square with a tightly fitting lid. This he presented to Mam with great pride. Sceptical but desperate, she agreed to give it a try and having hacked the round lid off the orange and blue tin she thrust it in the oven before refitting the box lid.

Embedded in embers, it was then 'clamped' round the sides and top with more hot ashes and an expectant and salivating audience waited patiently whilst the 'approx 45 minutes' ticked by on the silver time piece suspended from Dads watch chain. With much spitting on fingers and the assistance of a damp rag, the oven lid was prized off to appreciative gasps. Impressive layers of crisp golden pastry stretched heavenward and rich Oxo gravy oozed and trickled tantalisingly down the side of the pie tin. Served with tinned marrowfat peas and a mashing of King Edwards, it was indeed a feast fit for royalty. Scraping the last dregs encrusted to the pie tin, was a pleasure that fell to me.

Even our future King, Prince Charles, was a convert, surprising many when heard to declare on the wireless that he "remembered eating Frey Bentos until it came out of my ears". This led us to assume that he had an even greater share than the ordinary eared person.

Whilst Mam was in the 'send-us-wools' line of business, she snipped the buttons off the garments to lighten their weight before posting. On a wet day my job was to collect all the buttons and match them into sets of five or six. Dad cut finger length strips of white card and passed them to Mam who, braced with a needle and thread, impaled them in place. It was blunting work for a needle so Mam invested in a silver thimble to protect her "prodding" finger. Once carded up, they filled a basket along with other millinery merchandise which Dad would have sent away to Cheetham Hill in Manchester for.

Elastic, hooks and eyes, thimbles and lace, found ready customers amongst the "make do and mend" fraternity of the less financially fortified families.

On Saturdays, the field either knocked off early or didn't pick at all, depending on the state of the market. This heralded a trip into Evesham where there was a small market and a variety of country shops. While Dad and Nos Nos crouched down with their backs to the wall of the establishments, guarding the baskets of shopping and enjoying a leisurely smoke, Mam gossiped and nattered her way down each queue to the counter at the butcher's, the baker's and the tobacconist's. Purchases completed, we would all jump on Dad's cart and spin off homewards at a spanking trot causing the cobs chest and flanks to whiten with sweat, only to be drawn up sharply to a steaming halt when we reached home.

En route, it was common to see other Travellers on similar missions. Dressed in an old fashioned and pleasing array of mismatched garments and fabrics, they were nevertheless easily identified amongst other Gypsies, many by name, or nickname.

Broth-head, Snowy, Fish face, Hotpot, Whippet, Scar face and Stumpy were all well known and hollered or waved accordingly, exchanging exaggerated sniggers and smiles. Wives and children, ringletted and curled, nodded or waved, enjoying a day "off the field" in their going out finery.

13
As the Birds Sing

Our stopping place near to the railway line at Eckington was a footpath away from Lower Strensham and well within shadow of Bredon Hill. On fine evenings, Dad and Uncle would walk me on their shoulders up to Parsons Folly, a small stone tower built years earlier by the squire of Kemerton as a summer house. From here we surveyed the countryside laid out like a patchwork below, and through their usual pipe smoke haze pointed out familiar landmarks and stopping places. I wriggled my toes in the wild thyme and enjoyed the golden gorse blossoms, marvelling at the amount of rabbit droppings clustered on the short cropped grass. Years later, I fuelled Dads pipe with this material and marvelled at how well it made his pipe draw when disguised on top with a 'rubbing' of twist.

Having slithered and shuffled back down the hill, Dad had one more trick up his sleeve before bedtime.

Consulting his fob watch, he made back for home via the level crossing on the old railway line. Then, drawing two old ship half-pennys from his pocket, he set them both on the shiny metal railway lines and retired to the safety of the hedge bank, just as a rumbling could be heard in the distance. Whistle blowing, the train thundered past and as it receded into the distance we crept forward to see if the penny-crushing experiment had worked. The halfpenny was now wafer thin and equal to the size of an old penny. Dad retrieved both, and back at the campfire, he produced a tiny fret saw and proceeded to trim away the excess metal from each copper disc leaving two perfect little doves, which he polished to a sparkling shine with wood ash and Brasso. Nestling in the palm of his hand they looked handsome as the firelight caught their surface.

Mam wasn't best pleased, saying hadn't he, "More sense than to teach a baby to play on a railway line" and, "When 'is back was turned she'd be trying the caper for 'erself".

Sensing a domestic dawning, Uncle Norris pretended to fly the doves through the air by tapping a hole through each and attaching fishing line.

"Two little love birds sitting in a tree" he chanted in a last ditch attempt at humour.

Mam's caustic reply was "With one auld fool, I don't need thee".

Dad must have thought it over during the night, or maybe he wanted to alleviate Mam's concerns or the pea picking was nearly over and he had got restless. At any rate, before sundown he collected up his bantams and greased the waggon turntable and springs before retiring to bed.

The next day, in the mist of the morning, Dad had "put five miles under the 'osse's collar" before I had returned from the land of nod. I woke up to the ringing of hooves and the rumble of iron shod wheels on a metalled road.

The view both fore and aft showed wayside hedgerows and verges bedecked in bridal splendour. Late May blossom, heavily scented and elder flower in delicate whites and creams companioned "old ladies lace" waist high and fragile.

"We'm off strawberrying" informed Mam as we sped along, taking delight in the beauty of the day.

Of an evening, Mam would instruct Dad to collect some elder flower for her batter bathed fritter making. "Smell da flowers is it you'm wanting?" No complaints over this chore as the batter dipped blossoms were fast fried in fat to form filigree fringes then served still sizzling and plated with sharp lemon juice and sugar crystal.

With our journey punctuated via stopping places such as Brockeridge Green, Slades Green, Cobb Cross and Dymock (of Daffodil fame) we finally reached Much Marcle, pulling up a side lane past the Slip Inn.

This hostelry was named after a remarkable landslip which occurred in the 1500s when Much Marcle's hill went a wandering — "rousing itself as it were, out of a sleep... and for three days together, pushing and shoving its body forward with a horrible roaring noise and overturning everything in it's path, to the astonishment of bystanders". The chapel was overthrown and hedges, trees and cattle destroyed. A similar surge of nature to the Severn bore, a phenominum which I found so fascinating, back at Upton.

In 1840, during the ploughing of ancient pasture on the site of the land slip, called 'The Wonder', the bell of the old chapel was finally unearthed and returned to the villagers. Even up until Victorian times visitors came to view 'The Wonder' and the village even today has a certain mystic notoriety.

Little did we know then that its notoriety would increase for more chilling reasons, but unlike Fred and Rose West, Mam and Dad confined their activities to strawberry picking.

Content to move up and down the straw canopied rows on one knee, pinching off and punneting the lush fresh fruit with its finger staining juice and distinctive aroma of summer, was pleasant and lucrative labour.

Nothing says summer quite like a strawberry.

We sampled the wares most evenings served in little dishes with sugar and tinned cream.

The *gorgias** opted for broad brimmed hats, the Gypsies mostly toiled bare headed, sun browned arms moving with a tireless ease and grace which is so much a characteristic of their race.

Dad's brylcream melted down his face in rich rivulets to be absorbed by his *diklo** like a candle wick.

Each berry had to be rapidly checked for ripeness: if its tip was still white, it would not be as ripe as it should be. Some shyer berries lurked beneath the leaves, an experienced hand needed to deftly sweep beneath the leaves, locating at a touch.

Not then the large factory farms of today, but rather individual farms under one estate or small country holdings, husband and wife concerns, eking out a living with 'a bit of this an' that', produce supplying local grocers or sold on a formica-topped table, shaded by a fringed parasol from the entrance to the property or at the kitchen back door.

Dad preferred the latter and Gypsy families had their own particular properties that they'd call at regularly year after year.

Towards the end of the season, when the straw had been over trampled and the plants looked as tousled as a school boys hair, they would be speedily stripped of all the remaining berries and the harvest of over-ripes and misshaped despatched to a jam factory to be boiled in vats and deluged in sugar then racked on to shop shelves.

Around this time, two new supermarkets emerged – Fine Fare (the local branch had 12 hand baskets and 6 trolleys) and the Co-op who issued their customers with a dividend number. Mam's was 4711, like her favourite cologne. Later, like Green Shield, they issued stamps which could be redeemed in exchange for merchandise. Both stores were self-service, which created quite a stir. For those Travellers unable to read and write it posed a greater challenge as they had hither too been able to rely on the services of the shop assistant to select their requirements.

On the last day of strawberrying, Dad collected his money. Part of his wages included a pretty trio of 'golden aureoles' bantams which he carried home in a sack then lovingly polished with a silk scarf until their feathers shone. Chicks from these showy little performers would find a ready market amongst the old Romany families who appreciated something flashy and eye-catching.

While Mam and Dad had been working on the fields, Uncle Norris had had a visit from an over enthusiastic evangelist from the local chapel. "'E happened by an said as 'ow 'e was savin' arse-holes", said Uncle, proffering a slim religious tract printed on cheap paper. "Well 'e come to the right 'kin place then" said Dad, breaking into a wide grin and using the paper as a spill to light his pipe from the fire.

"I put 'e a-goin', 'e could 'av bin delations to the devil", Nos Nos warmed to his account "Hair down 'is back an more like a 'oman, an more 'kin tattoos than a sailor's bicep."

Further deliberation was interrupted by one of those unexpected yet drenching summer showers that persist even when the sun shines.

Taking temporary cover under mammoth burdock leaves, held aloft umberella style, we watched as the colourful arc of a rainbow formed.

The sun's rays caused steam to rise from a road only recently shimmering with a heat haze. Vapour rose from the lane in profusion as the moisture rapidly dried.

From beneath his large leaf, Dad reminded us that, legend had it, treasure lay at a rainbow's end. Mam said she reckoned it must be on the strawberry fields then, "Cos the old boy what's there had more *luvva** than he can shake a stick at".

As Dad heaped more wood on the fire and the flames rose to envelop the sooty black kettle, the longest day of the year approached.

Time had moved on and we had accompanied it on the road since that gentle spring of 1959, that apple blossom time, in the Vale of Evesham.

My parents had gone through a rite of passage – as the *gorgias** call it – and been transformed by the arrival of their daughter.

What we none of us realised then was that the world as we knew it was undergoing its own rite of passage. The days of waggon time were coming to an end more rapidly than we realised and with it, a transformation in the lives of Gypsy people. The challenges we had faced so far were to prove not as challenging as the adjustments that lay ahead and on that day of summer showers we were blessed to be veiled from the turn of events that was to meet us on the road ahead.

Romani
and Notes

Acoi – here
Annie and Lally – see the book *Born on the Straw*
Atchin tan – stopping place
Beng – devil
Bootying – working
Chavvy – child
Choomia – kiss
Chopping – exchanging
Chorred – stolen
Del – give
Dik – look, see
Diklo – neckerchief
Gorgia – non Gypsy
Gypsy cake – traditional Gypsy food
Juks – dogs
Kannis – hens
Kekauvi saster – kettle iron
Ladging – shameful; disgrace
Luvva – money
Mandy's – my
Meskie – tea
Mokadi – ritually unclean
Monging – begging
Mush – man, friend
Muskra – police officer
Parni – water
Patrins – trail signs
Praster – go for
Rakli – girl
Swegler – pipe
Vittles – food (victuals)
Yog – fire
Yokel muskra – country bobby
Yoks — eyes